What's Cooking in Children's Literature

Gwynne Spencer

PROFESSIONAL GROWTH SERIES®

A Publication of THE BOOK REPORT & LIBRARY TALK
Professional Growth Series

Linworth Publishing, Inc.
Worthington, Ohio

Library of Congress Cataloging-in-Publication Data

Spencer, Gwynne
    What's cooking in children's literature / Gwynne Spencer.
      p. cm.
    Includes bibliographical references.
    ISBN 1-58683-005-8 (perfect bound)
    1. Cookery. 2. Children's literature. I. Title.

    TX652 .S63 2000
    641.5--dc21

00-048137

Published by Linworth Publishing, Inc.
480 East Wilson Bridge Road, Suite L
Worthington, Ohio 43085

Copyright©2001 by Linworth Publishing, Inc.

Series Information:
    From The Professional Growth Series

ISBN 1-58683-005-8

5 4 3 2 1

Table of Contents

Table of Contents continued

Table of Contents continued

Table of Contents continued

Table of Contents continued

Table of Contents continued

Introduction

"Cooking in the classroom, and likewise in the library? You must be crazy!" I can hear people thinking. Well, there's no better way to connect young people and books than through their stomachs—and it doesn't have to make a big mess either. This cookbook is designed to help teachers and librarians engage in beneficial collaborations to bring reading to the lips of students in new and delightfully delicious ways. The more than 200 recipes offered here will tempt even the most reluctant reader of any age to nibble at a new book.

Why in the world would you want to even think about cooking together with kids? Isn't it easier, safer, and saner to just do it yourself and present the finished product to students? Of course, it's always easier to just whip up something and take it to school. Nevertheless, many of the recipes included in this book are fun and easy to do with students. The recipes enhance the process of learning so much that preparing them with students is definitely worth the effort and energy required. If, however, it's your professional opinion that it would be best to make the snack at home and take it to school all pretty and finished, then by all means do it. It's sort of like laminating—it's much easier done without children.

Among its educational advantages, cooking reinforces students' abilities to follow directions and hones their reading and math skills. Hands-on cooking experience also helps students visualize concepts of weight, length, volume, and other measurements, and allows them to improve their comprehension of time, color, and shape. Cooking encourages cooperation, and students feel a sense of accomplishment when together they finally produce an edible project. Make it easy on yourself: Use mixes and appliances, and make a finished version to serve when the recipe involves a process that won't be completed for a long time.

Every one of the recipes includes ties to at least one book you probably can find on your library shelf. Some recipes can be used with many books on the same topic. Most recipes require an electric appliance you can find in the teacher's lounge or at home, such as a microwave, blender, crockpot, toaster oven, electric skillet, or griddle. To make preparation a snap, many recipes use mixes or canned ingredients. Cooking can be messy, but if you lay down the rules and keep enforcing them, you will have fabulous results.

These recipes for snack time evolved

from the simple preferences of children whose main gastronomic requirements were (1) not being forced to eat foods that touch each other and (2) not having to eat anything that was previously alive. The main requirements for the snacks to be included in this book were that they tie to a children's book and that they be simple. If they were also cheap and easy to serve, that was all the better. If the youngsters liked them, the snacks earned more points. And if the teacher and students loved the related book in addition to the snack, the combination earned bonus points. If the snack looked great as well as tasted great, it made me eligible for the Martha Stewart Award. And if the other teachers wanted to know (a) how to make the snack and (b) how to get the book, it was a legend! In addition to my own recipes and those contributed by teachers and librarians, this humble cookbook also includes entries contributed by wildly famous and successful children's authors and illustrators. The unifying element is that they all pertain to reading in some integral way.

When planning a cooking activity, think collaboration. If the librarian is reading the book and introducing the idea, perhaps the teacher would want to plan the cooking activity in the classroom. Or if the teacher wants to culminate a unit with cooking, perhaps the library would be a grand place to share the cooking project with another class or the teachers. One of the best collaborations is for the teacher and librarian to help students develop their own recipes based on their favorite books, then type the recipes on a word processor, illustrate them, and make them into a unique cookbook.

Nothing in this book will win any awards for originality or healthfulness. All the recipes here are designed to feed 12 kids. You can double them or halve them easily. The recipes are fairly simple so you can get through the steps without having a nervous breakdown. These are all kid-tested recipes. And best of all, they each tie to a title that you can read while the little munchkins eat the snacks. Undoubtedly, at some point, every person who reads this book will say to himself or herself, "Gee, why didn't they include a recipe for XYZ to go with the book ABC?" Perhaps that's your opportunity to extend your cooking into writing! It also makes kids voracious perusers of cookbooks. These recipes are all pretty no-brainer and instant. Perhaps the hardest step will be figuring out how to transport them to the classroom.

Most snacks that youngsters make are going to be rife with germs. Obviously, students cooking in a classroom need to be taught NOT to lick their fingers and then handle food. They need to learn the necessity of hand washing and the niceties of sanitation for the safety of the group. Make it a rule that children cannot consume any batter with raw eggs in it, cannot lick fingers, cannot eat uncooked meat, and cannot handle uncooked chicken in any form (all the chicken in these recipes is precooked). Use only milk products that have been pasteurized and are not likely go bad in the amount of time allotted in any of these recipes. Cutting surfaces, spoons, bowls, and knives need to be sanitized with something pretty severe to kill germs. Don't take the chance of being a Typhoid Mary from lax sanitation.

If you are cooking anything together with youngsters, always keep in mind that they have approximately NO experience in their memory banks. They don't know (as you do) that hot oil spits when you put things in it. They don't know that things can catch fire on the stove in the blink of an eye. They don't know about metal's spectacular effects in a microwave. You need to anticipate all the things that can go wrong, especially when it comes to sharp objects like knives, skewers, large forks, and related "weapons." While much of the Montessori method is devoted to teaching children to handle knives and other lethal weapons with respect, restraint, and responsibility, most non-Montessori students haven't got a clue. Given the chance, the minute you turn your back, they'll be dueling with the carving knives, trying to poke each other's arms with the barbecue fork, or squirting ketchup at each other as if they had some sort of genetic memory of *Animal House* food fights. Some rules you might want to post before cooking (and enforce rigorously while cooking) include the following:

1. No fooling around during cooking or OUT YOU GO.
2. Utensils and tools for cooking may only be used for cooking. Anyone who wants to reenact dueling scenes from *The Princess Bride* or stabbing scenes from *Jaws* is "O-U-T-OUT," as Ramona Quimby would say.
3. Cooking is not for just the results, but for the learning along the way.
4. The reason they're called INSTRUCTIONS and not SUGGESTIONS is that you HAVE to follow them.
5. Do it right—or you don't get to do it at all.
6. No more than three kids in a group, no less than three feet between groups, and no more than three steps in a process.

Cooking with youngsters requires keeping a lid on things and not letting exuberance turn into craziness. Discipline and control are vital to the process. Do not tolerate even the slightest infraction of safety rules. Be absolutely firm in your insistence that students exhibit good behavior or lose out on the chance to participate in the cooking activity.

Brainstorm with students about food that ties to books. You'll find them really cooking up a storm if you ask them to think ingredient by ingredient. For example, sugar wafer cookies, with their little tread marks, would make great city walls. Healthy Advantage® ginger animal crackers come with elephants, lions, hippos, bears, and more. You could populate a whole realm with Sesame Street® characters, Keebler Elf Grahams®, and other unique crackers and cookies. You could also get creative with Pepperidge Farm® Butter Thins butterfly-shaped crackers, and Melba toast would make terrific wagon wheels with a pretzel right through the middle. Several forms of breadsticks and pretzels can be "glued" together with peanut butter, honey, or icing to form walls, bridges, log cabins, and forts. Keebler waffle bowls can hold just about anything that's not runny (e.g., ice cream, pudding, pie, cake batter, stew, chili). Nilla® wafers don't just come in vanilla any more; they come in rainbow and chocolate flavors as well. You can find alphabet- and number-shaped cookies and crackers as well. At groceries, you can find gummy snakes, worms, and fish, and candy stores offer a greater variety of gummy critters. Asking kids to think about "What looks like a wall?" encourages divergent thinking and true creativity. "What can we use for the ocean?" will cause kids to mentally run through the supermarket thinking of edible possibilities.

This book aims to help you begin your adventures in playing with food. In addition to having fun cooking, learning about measuring, and following directions, youngsters (and grownups) plowing through this book might want to plan a Reading Fair Event, which is sort of like Science Fair except that the exhibits all tie to children's books. Students would enjoy having the chance to show off their edible projects, and perhaps they may even want to make one recipe for show and one for nibbling. Some of the recipes that are not edible, but rather intended to have a visual effect, might form the core of a Reading-Eating Fair in your school.

A cautionary note before you begin: It's great to cook with students, but you have to beware of food allergies. In this litigious day and age, it never hurts to be too careful. Sometimes in the excitement of cooking, youngsters will forget they have anaphylactic reactions to eggs, wheat, or milk. You really don't want kids tasting things that might kill them, so it is a good idea to look at their allergy records before you cook. It's easy to avoid problems with simple lists of who might be allergic to what and choose recipes accordingly. Students with allergies *hate* it when they are singled out, so this checking is best done beforehand. Furthermore, children who are afraid of being ostracized from the cooking activity might actually *lie* about their allergies and then things could really get challenging for you. The most common allergic reactions are to milk, eggs, wheat, and chocolate, but lots of potential offenders are lurking in the culinary shadows. Sometimes you can substitute or leave out a minor ingredient, but sometimes you can't. If in doubt, err on the side of safety and choose another recipe.

If you've read this far, by now you're probably chomping at the bit to start cooking. The recipes are arranged alphabetically by book title because that is the simplest way to do it, and simple is always best. The Index lists them by book title, author, and recipe name as well, so you can navigate the 200-plus entries without difficulty. As Julia Child's dog would say, "Bone Appétit!"

—*Gwynne Spencer*

The Special Cooking Vocabulary

If you've read the *Amelia Bedelia* books, you know the perils of literally following cooking directions (as when she "dresses the chicken"). Many words used in cooking processes have a new contextual meaning that kids do not understand. Take the time to explain and explicate terms such as *cube, cut, chop, dice, blend, mix, mash, moosh, smash, crush, peel, bake, nuke,* and *stir.* Never take anything for granted. The easiest rule of thumb is to assume you are dealing with newly arrived immigrants from Mars who have no clue what a microwave is or how to operate it. They have never seen an oven and might mistake it for a doghouse. Take time to go over everything. It's all part of the learning experience.

One of our favorite books is *The Dumb Bunnies* by Sue Denim, who is a very good friend of Dav Pilkey. In this fine piece of literature, the Dumb Bunnies rely heavily on one appliance—the Nukemaster microwave—thus introducing to children's literature the term *nuke* as a cooking process. Most students these days know about the dangers of standing too near the microwave and innately understand the term "nuke" as a shorthand phrase for "cook in the microwave."

In addition to the indispensable microwave, some other kitchen tools you might want to round up include the following:

bowls of various sizes and colors	toaster oven	popcorn popper
wooden spoons	microwave	noodle maker
serving utensils	blender	electric skillet/fry pan
pancake turner	knives of various kinds, small for small kids	grater
cookie sheets	cutting boards	can opener
measuring cups	spaghetti rake	serving platters
wire whisks	colander/strainer	pot holders
rolling pins	cheese cloth	Ziploc® plastic bags
pie tins	rice steamer	Pyrex® or other heat-resistant glass
muffin pans	juice squeezer	custard cups
ice cube trays	ice cream maker	(6-ounce)

Clean up is always easier if you don't have dishes to wash. Use paper plates every chance you get. If lots of cooking is going on in school, you may want to bulk buy items at a discount warehouse to save tons of money.

Recipes

GROSS, GREEN, SLIMY, GIANT TEETH to go with

Abiyoyo: An African Lullaby by Pete Seeger, illustrated by Michael Hays, Simon & Schuster: ISBN 0027814904 (hc), Aladdin: ISBN 0689718101 (pbk).

■ Abiyoyo is the giant who is tricked into lying down and zapped with a magic wand after being exhausted by the magician's son. Abiyoyo has horrible green, slimy teeth because he never brushes them. Here's how to make edible replicas of his gross dentition.

Ingredients
1 package Doritos® tortilla chips
1 container fresh guacamole
grated Monterey Jack or Colby cheese

Directions
On a paper plate, spread each tortilla chip with some guacamole, sprinkle with grated cheese and arrange in a "mouth" shape.

MAGICAL ZUCCHINI AIRPLANES to go with

Airport by Byron Barton, HarperTrophy: ISBN 0064431452 (pbk), 0690041691 (lb). Also good with The *Little Red Plane* by Ken Wilson-Max, Cartwheel Books: ISBN 0439136539 (bd), or *Planes* by Byron Barton, HarperCollins: ISBN 0694011665 (bd).

■ Students might have so much fun making these airplanes that they won't want to eat them right away. Nevertheless, they will love eating them after reading their vicarious flying adventures.

Ingredients
12 cheese sticks
12 grapes, green or red
almond slivers
12 carrot "coins"
pretzel sticks

Other
toothpicks

Directions
Cut cheese sticks into 2-inch pieces, each of which will become the fuselage of an airplane. Using a table knife, make two slits in the sides of the cheese for the wings to be inserted, then insert almond sliver wings. Cut grapes in half for the cockpit and set gently on top. Use more almond slivers for the tail rudders. For the propeller, use a knife to make little slits in the sides of the carrot coin and insert almond slivers for the blades. Push a pretzel stick through the middle of the propeller (easier if you make the hole with a toothpick first) and insert into the front of the fuselage. For the landing gear, insert two pretzel sticks under the cockpit/grape. Clear! (That's what pilots yell before they start the engine.)

AUSTRALIAN VEGEMITE SANDWICHES to go with
Alexander and the Terrible Horrible No Good Very Bad Day by Judith Viorst, illustrated by Ray Cruz, Aladdin: ISBN 0689711735 (pbk); Atheneum: 0689300727 (lb).

■ Vegemite comes in jars (a little jar goes a very long way), and personally I think it tastes like shoe polish, but maybe that's because I was born in the wrong hemisphere. If you can't find it in the supermarket, ask at the food co-op. You can also use Vegemite in connection with other Australian stories, such as *Koala Lou* by Mem Fox, illustrated by Pamela Lofts, Harcourt Brace: 0152000763 (pbk), 0152005021 (lb); *One Woolly Wombat* by Rod Trinca, illustrated by Kerry Argent, Kane Miller: ISBN 0916291103 (pbk); and *Possum Magic* by Mem Fox, illustrated by Julie Vivas, Harcourt Brace: 0152005722 (hc), 0152632247 (pbk). In Viorst's story, as the day gets worse and worse, Alexander threatens to go to Australia. He probably wouldn't if he knew he'd have to eat Vegemite.

Ingredients
1 tiny jar of Vegemite
sandwich bread
jelly
cream cheese

marshmallow fluff
slices of kiwi fruit
alfalfa or bean sprouts

Directions
Spread Vegemite thinly on each slice of bread. Add jelly, cream cheese, marshmallow fluff, sprouts, or even slices of kiwi fruit. If you can't find Vegemite, choose another recipe.

LIMA BEAN MONKEY VOMIT CASSEROLE to go with
Alexander and the Terrible Horrible No Good Very Bad Day by Judith Viorst, illustrated by Ray Cruz, Aladdin: ISBN 0689711735 (pbk); Atheneum: ISBN 0689300727 (lb).

■ If your students hate lima beans as much as Alexander does, they'll hate this recipe. You could also use it with *A Bad Case of the Stripes* by David Shannon, Scholastic: ISBN 0590929976 (hc), in which the little girl character loves lima beans.

Ingredients
1 package frozen lima beans
1 can chopped tomatoes, juice and all

1 cup bread cubes
Parmesan cheese

Directions
Mix all ingredients together and put into an ovenproof casserole dish. Top with Parmesan cheese. Bake at 350°F for about 45 minutes, until bubbly. You could also make into individual casseroles using recycled cat food cans that have gone through the dishwasher.

CHESHIRE CAT SMILES

to go with *Alice in Wonderland* by Lewis Carroll, illustrated by John Tenniel, Grossett and Dunlap: ISBN 0448060043 (hc).

■ Alice watches the Cheshire cat disappear in the tree until all that's left is its smile. These snacks are all smiles with no cat, no tree.

Ingredients
4 or 5 apples with red skin
peanut butter
tiny marshmallows

Directions
Cut apples into wedges about one-finger thick on the outside tapering to nothing at the middle. These are the "lips" of the smile, so you want nice red apples. Spread one side of each apple slice with peanut butter. Between two peanut-buttered sides put a row of marshmallows to look like teeth. Smoosh lightly so the teeth stay straight.

MAD HATTER TREACLE TREATS

to go with *Alice in Wonderland* by Lewis Carroll, illustrated by John Tenniel, Grossett and Dunlap: ISBN 0448060043 (hc). There are lots of different versions of *Alice*. This one has the "original" illustrations.

■ Revisiting Alice's tea party is a great excuse to try out different weird finger foods. Since nobody seems to know what a "treacle treat" actually IS, this ought to pass for the real thing.

Ingredients
3 shredded carrots
1 small can mandarin oranges, drained
1 small container plain cream cheese
1/2 teaspoon ginger (dried powder)
12 slices white bread

Other
cookie cutters

Directions
Use cookie cutters to cut bread into shapes such as diamonds, clubs, spades, hearts, bunnies, or hats. Moosh other ingredients together with a wooden spoon in a bowl. Spread mixture on bread. Serve on paper lace doilies.

NACHO MACHO to go

with *Alice Nizzy Nazzy: The Witch of Santa Fe* by Tony Johnston, illustrated by Tomie dePaola, Putnam: ISBN 069811650X (pbk), 0399227881 (lb).

■ A witch named Alice steals Manuela's sheep in this Southwest version of *Baba Yaga*. Instead of cooking up the feisty little girl in her cauldron, the mean *bruja* would have done better to whip up this traditional New Mexico treat.

Ingredients
6 cups Colby or Monterey Jack cheese, shredded
2 bags Fritos® or blue corn tortilla chips
olive slices
canned chili
green onion, chopped

Directions
Spread a layer of chips on a paper plate for each person. Sprinkle cheese (about one-half cup per child) over chips. Nuke for 30-60 seconds until cheese melts. If you nuke it too long, the cheese will get rubbery. Add olives, chili, and onions to taste.

HAWAIIAN CLIFFHANGERS to go

with *Aloha, Dolores* by Barbara Samuels, DK Publishing: ISBN 0789425084 (hc).

■ Dolores plans to win a trip to Hawaii because of her cat Duncan's love of Meow Munchies. In spite of her earnest enthusiasm, things work out somewhat differently for both of them, but throughout the book, Dolores sips these treats.

Ingredients
1 can coconut milk (look in the Asian foods section)
water
pineapple juice

Other
ice cube trays
paper umbrellas
tall clear glasses (plastic is fine)

Directions
Mix coconut milk with two parts water and freeze into ice cubes ahead of time. When you are ready to enjoy the story, fill each glass with coconut ice cubes, add canned pineapple juice, and then top off your Aloha Drinks with a little paper umbrella. Sip while you listen to Hawaiian music and dream of the trip you're going to win to the islands.

THE DIRTY BABY'S MOTHER'S ANGEL FOOD CAKE treat to keep

away imps from *Alpha and the Dirty Baby* by Brock Cole, Sunburst: ISBN 0374403570 (pbk); Econo-Clad: 0613095081 (lb).

■ When the imps come into the house and take over, the mother is getting ready to make angel food cake. Then the imps make everything all dirty and ugly, but eventually it all turns back to normal. Enjoy eating angel food cake the way imps would love it—with "dirt" on it!

Ingredients
1 ready-made angel food cake
1 can ready-made chocolate icing

Directions
Put a can of chocolate icing into the center of the angel food cake. Let kids tear off pieces of the cake and dip it into the icing. This has absolutely NO nutritional value but is certain to keep away the imps as long as the cake and chocolate hold out. You could substitute chocolate pudding (it has to be brown, to represent the dirt) if you are determined to add at least a smidgen of redeeming value.

GREAT BIG OWWY THORN IN THE PAW

to go with *Andy and the Lion* by James Daugherty, Viking: ISBN 0140502777 (pbk); Econo-Clad: 0833529951 (lb).

■ In this retelling of *Androcles and the Lion*, a tale of courage and compassion, the lion has a humongous thorn in its paw and Andy removes it, thus engendering the lion's eternal friendship and allegiance.

Ingredients
3 cans refrigerated biscuits, preferably Pillsbury Grands!® (24 total)
12 pieces candy corn

Directions
Cut 12 biscuits into quarters, roll into little balls to look like "lions toes," then pinch and shape four "toes" onto one side of a whole biscuit to make it look like a big lion's foot. Bake at 350˚F for about 10 minutes until browned. Stick a piece of candy corn (the thorn) into the "pad" of the lion's paw after the biscuits are cool.

ANNA BANANA'S FEARLESS BANANA TREATS to go

with *Anna Banana* by Lenore Blegvad, illustrated by Erik Blegvad, Aladdin: ISBN 068971114X (pbk); Econo-Clad: 0808592319

■ These snacks are destined to make you as fearless as Anna Banana is on the playground!

Ingredients
12 bananas
1 jar peanut butter
1 jar Miracle Whip®

Directions
Peel bananas, and then slice them lengthwise. Cover each half generously with peanut butter, then add dollops of Miracle Whip. Serve with plastic forks because this is a messy snack.

CORN CAKES FOR LURING CATS HOME

to go with *Annie and the Wild Animals* by Jan Brett, Houghton Mifflin: ISBN 0395510066 (pbk), 0395378001 (lb).

■ Annie's cat has run away and she tries to lure a new pet with these yummy corn cakes.

Ingredients
3 tablespoons melted butter
2 cans 15-ounce cream-style corn
1 bag frozen corn (not on the cob) thawed and drained
1 package Jiffy corn muffin mix
1 8-ounce container sour cream
3 large eggs
2 tablespoons minced onion
1 teaspoon dried parsley flakes
1 tablespoon honey

Directions
Put cupcake papers into a muffin tin. Mix all ingredients together in a big bowl until smooth. Pour into muffin tin, filling each cup about 2/3 full. Bake at 350˚F for about 40 minutes or until tops are browned.

YUMMY BUGS to go with
Are You a Ladybug? by
Judy Allen, illustrated by
Tudor Humphries,
Larousse Kingfisher
Chambers: ISBN
0753452413 (hc), *The
Grouchy Ladybug* by Eric
Carle, HarperCollins:
ISBN 0064434508 (pbk);
HarperFestival:
069401320X (bd); or
Ladybug, Ladybug by
Ruth Brown, Puffin: ISBN
0140545433 (pbk).

■ Making edible ladybugs is not only fun, it's delicious. If you decide to use this with *The Grouchy Ladybug*, every time the ladybug says, "Hey, you want to fight?" the kids could substitute, "Hey, you want a licking?" and lick their ice cream.

Ingredients
pink ice cream or frozen yogurt
blueberries
Smucker's® Magic Shell ice cream topping
mini chocolate chips or M&M's®
ice cream cones

Directions
On top of an ice cream scoop of pink ice cream or frozen yogurt firmly scooped onto the cone (so it doesn't fall out on the floor), add two blueberries for eyes, draw a stripe of chocolate syrup across the scoop just a little past midway to delineate the top of the body, then add a perpendicular line to the end of the scoop (you're making a *T*). Put on mini chocolate chips or M&M's for the "dots" on the ladybug's shell.

BABY BIRD ZUCCHINI NESTS to go with *Are You My Mother?* by P. D. Eastman, Random House: ISBN 0394800184 (hc).

■ The baby bird falls out of its nest and goes in search of its mother. Maybe it wouldn't have fallen out of this yummy nest.

Ingredients

12 zucchini, grated and squeezed until they don't "cry" anymore
1 cup grated Parmesan cheese
1 beaten egg
1 small minced onion (you can leave this out if students don't like onions)
1 cup flour
1 cup vegetable oil
6 hard-boiled eggs cut in half
sunflower seed kernels for eyes
1 bunch fresh parsley
almond slices

Directions

Mix together zucchini, cheese, egg, onion, and flour in a big bowl. When well mixed, form into little nest shapes in the palm of your hand, making an indentation where the "baby bird" will go. In a electric skillet, heat vegetable oil to spitting-hot, add one nest at a time, so the oil doesn't splash; usually about six at a time will cook fastest. Cook covered about five minutes until brown and crispy on the bottom. Remove to a cookie sheet (you might put a few layers of paper towels down to absorb oil), and put in a 300° oven while you finish cooking all the nests. When they're all cooked, you're ready to add the "baby bird," which is one-half of a hard-boiled egg, flat side down, with an almond slice beak, two sunflower kernels for eyes, and a sprig of parsley for the "hair" or whatever you call the stuff on the top of his head.

PURR-FECT ANGEL BISCUITS to go

with *Barn Kitty* by June Kirkpatrick, illustrated by Lori Peterson, Azro Press: ISBN 0966023951 (pbk).

■ The barn kitty becomes an angel in the sky at the end of this story; the biscuits are as light and feathery as an angel cloud.

Ingredients

1 package active dry yeast
2 tablespoons very warm water
5 cups all purpose flour
1 teaspoon baking soda
3 teaspoons baking powder
2 tablespoons sugar
1 teaspoon salt
1 cup shortening
2 cups buttermilk

Other

cookie cutters

Directions

Dissolve yeast in water. Sift all dry ingredients into a large bowl. Cut in shortening. Add buttermilk, then yeast mixture. Stir until thoroughly moistened, turn onto floured board and knead a minute or two. No rising is required. Roll out to desired thickness (1/2-inch is good) and cut into rounds (use cookie cutters for fun shapes). Brush with melted butter and bake on ungreased baking sheet at 400°F for 12 to 15 minutes until lightly browned. Baked biscuits freeze beautifully. Makes about 24. Contributed by the author.

INCREDIBLE, SLIMY OOBLECK to go with

Bartholomew and the Oobleck by Dr. Seuss, Random House: ISBN 0394800753 (hc) or with *It Looked Like Spilt Milk* by Charles G. Shaw, HarperCollins: 069400491X (board book).

■ King Derwin of Didd orders up something new from his magicians—oobleck. Nobody knows exactly what "oobleck" is, but it's really hard to contain. This stuff is pretty close to the original. It's also inedible, but we include it here because it's such a nifty recipe. Be sure to warn the kids not to eat this (it's not toxic, but they'll gag). If you use this with *It Looked Like Spilt Milk*, you can let it spread onto squares of blue paper.

Ingredients
1 tablespoon laundry borax
1 small container Elmer's® glue, any size
food coloring

Other
2 empty plastic liter soda bottles
Ziploc® bags

Directions
Put borax into one soda bottle. Add one cup water, put on cap, and shake well. In the other soda bottle, combine glue with an equal amount of water. Add food coloring. In a bowl (preferably clear), dramatically combine one cup of glue mix and one cup of borax mix. Add a little at a time, and stir with a finger all the while. In about 30 seconds, it globs up. Grab the oobleck in your hand, pick it up, squeeze out the water, keep patting your hand dry on a towel (not your shirt, please) and soon the oobleck is "done." The more you work with it the drier it becomes. You can keep it in a Ziploc bag.

THE BAD GUY'S EDIBLE CROCODILES to go
with *Bill and Pete* by Tomie dePaola, Putnam: ISBN 0399206469 (hc), PaperStar: 0698114000 (pbk).

■ These look like little crocodiles, which is what William Everett Crocodile is, after all.

Ingredients
1/2 cup peanut butter
1 12-ounce bag marshmallows
green food coloring
almond slivers

4 cups Rice Krispies®, Cheerios®, or any corn flakes cereal

Directions
Nuke peanut butter and marshmallows in a glass bowl until melted. Add food color until it's a lovely green. Add cereal. Mix together. Butter your hands and form mixture into long thin cucumber shapes. Don't forget to make the tail pointy and the snout sort of pointy. Add almond sliver eyes and teeth. Let the snacks rest in the refrigerator until your ready to eat them.

BLUEBERRY MUFFINS to go with *Blueberries for Sal* by Robert McCloskey, Viking: ISBN 0670175919 (hc), 014050169X (pbk).

■ You're sure to find muffins among the favorite treats Sal and her mother might make with the blueberries they picked. If you totally want to just bail out on cooking, you can always find blueberry muffins in the bakery section of the grocery. Furthermore, an amazing number of blueberry muffin mixes are available in the baking aisle.

Ingredients
1 3/4 cups flour
2 1/2 teaspoons baking powder
1/2 teaspoon salt
1/2 cup sugar
3/4 cup milk

1 egg
1/3 cup melted butter
1 1/2 cups fresh or frozen blueberries
1/2 teaspoon cinnamon

Directions
Combine flour, baking powder, salt, and all but one tablespoon of sugar in a large bowl. Combine milk and egg in a small bowl. Add egg mixture to flour mixture with melted butter. Stir just until blended. Stir in blueberries. Put batter in cupcake papers in muffin pan. Combine remaining one tablespoon of sugar and cinnamon in a small bowl and sprinkle over muffins. Bake for 15-20 minutes at 350°F or until a toothpick inserted in the center comes out clean.

LITTLE SAL'S LITTLE PIES

to go with *Blueberries for Sal* by Robert McCloskey, Viking: ISBN 0670175919 (hc), 014050169X (pbk).

■ While picking blueberries, Little Sal and Little Bear meet up and surprise each other. Later, Sal and her mother make blueberry treats. We never find out what the mother bear and the cub do with their blueberries, though.

Ingredients
1 package ready-made pie crusts
2 cans blueberry pie filling
1 large container whipped cream or Cool Whip®

Directions
Line each cup of a 12-cup muffin tin with a 6-inch circle of pie crust. Don't cut off the excess, as this will become the top crust of the pie. Fill each little pie about halfway with canned blueberry pie filling (this will take two cans) Fold excess pie crust over top of filling, bake for 25 minutes at 350°F until crust browns. Serve with whipped cream or Cool Whip® topping. If time does not allow for baking pies, you could also use ready-made shortcake and spoon the blueberry filling and whipped cream onto the little cakes.

BREAD AND JAM TREATS

to go with *Bread and Jam for Frances* by Russell Hoban, illustrated by Lillian Hoban, HarperCollins: ISBN 0060223596 (hc), 0064430960 (pbk).

■ Frances goes on a diet of only bread and jam. Most kids know grape jelly, and that's about it! Ask each class member to bring a different kind of jam or jelly to really open this up to the many flavor possibilities. (*To make homemade strawberry jam, see the* **Quick Strawberry Jam** *entry.*)

Ingredients
fresh soft white Bread
jam of various flavors

Other
knives or cookie cutters

Directions
Spread a different kind of jam generously on a piece of white bread. Top with another piece of bread. Cut crusts off (Frances would like it better that way), and if you want, cut out fancy shapes with the cookie cutter. Would Frances eat the leftover pieces? You bet!

BROWN AS A BEAR BISCUITS to go with

Brown Bear, Brown Bear, What Do You See? by Bill Martin, Jr., illustrated by Eric Carle, Holt: ISBN 0805017445 (hc), 0805002014 (lb), 0805047905 (board book).

■ These edible brown bears are as memorable as the refrain from this classic book.

Ingredients

one can biscuits to make one big "bear" (most come eight to a can)
butter or nonstick cooking spray
1 teaspoon instant coffee
2 tablespoons brown sugar
Hershey's Kisses® (for eyes and ears)

Directions

Coat glass pie dish with butter or nonstick cooking spray. In the greased dish, smoosh six buttermilk biscuits out of a can into one big biscuit. Turn out dough onto cookie sheet. Cut one more biscuit in half to be the ears. Attach at "10 o'clock" and "two o'clock" positions. Put one biscuit in the middle of the face to be the muzzle. Brush the whole bear biscuit with a thin paint of brown sugar, water, and instant coffee to give it a nice, brown bear look. Bake about 12 minutes at 350°F. While still warm, put on two Hershey kisses for eyes, and insert two Hershey's Kisses into the ears for the centers, pointy side down. Wait till it cools down to eat or the melted chocolate will run all over and make a mess. Alternatively, if you want to make individual brown bears, have each kid start with a Pillsbury Grands! Biscuit (they're huge) and add pieces of another Grands! for the muzzle and ears, using chocolate chips for the eyes instead of a kiss.

SUPER LONG-LASTING BUBBLES to go with
Bubble Bubble by Mercer Mayer, Rainbird: ISBN 1879920034 (hc), or *Bubble Trouble* by Mary Packard, illustrated by Elena Kuckank, Scholastic: 0590485134 (pbk).

■ Both stories are about making long-lasting bubbles. This recipe is the "secret formula" children's museums use in their bubble trays.

Ingredients
1 part Karo® syrup
3 parts Joy liquid detergent or clear Ivory
8 parts water

Other
a 40-inch-long piece of string or yarn per child (the length of their arm span)
2 soda straws

Directions
Mix ingredients together in a shallow pan. To make bubble wands, loop 40-inch-long string or yarn threaded through soda straws (you hold the straws out to the sides forming a sort of square of the string). Dip bubble wands into mixture and make bubbles outdoors. The syrup attracts insects, so if you have any problems in your area with killer bees, I wouldn't do this outside.

WILBERTA'S WHISKER-LICKIN' CARROT CAKE

from *Buckley and Wilberta* by Hope Slaughter, illustrated by Susan Torrence, Red Hen Press: ISBN 0931093155 (hc)

■ A tall, slender rabbit named Wilberta and her best friend, Buckley, a short, pudgy hedgehog, celebrate Wilberta's birthday with her favorite kind of cake. Wilberta says follow the "Rabbit Party" illustration to assemble the cake. Contributed by Hope Slaughter.

Ingredients
2 cups sugar
1 1/2 cups cooking oil
4 large eggs
2 1/4 cups flour
2 teaspoons baking soda
2 teaspoons ground cinnamon
1 teaspoon salt
1 small can crushed pineapple
3 cups grated carrots

Icing
1 1/2 pounds powdered sugar
12 ounces cream cheese
2 1/4 sticks butter
3 teaspoons vanilla
2 1/4 cups Buckley's Super Nutty Pecans
1 1/2 cups crushed pineapple well drained

Other
8-inch round pans or cupcake tins

Directions
Cream together sugar and cooking oil. Beat eggs well and then add to sugar mixture. Sift together flour, baking soda, ground cinnamon, and salt, and fold into sugar mixture. Add crushed pineapple and "Wilberta's garden-fresh" grated carrots. Pour batter into two prepared 8-inch round pans or cupcake tins. Bake at 325°F for 40 minutes. To make icing, combine powdered sugar, cream cheese, butter, vanilla, pecans, and crushed pineapple.

MAX'S EARTHWORM CAKE WITH CATERPILLAR ICING AND RED HOT SQUIRTERS

from *Bunny Cakes* by
Rosemary Wells, Dial:
ISBN 0803721439 (hc),
Puffin: 0140566678 (pbk).

■ Max wants to make *his* kind of cake for his grandmother. Ruby, of course, is horrified and wants to make *her* kind of cake (*see the following recipe*), but Max, as always, does things his way.

Ingredients
1 box devil's food cake mix (make according to package directions, but bake in a large round bottomed mixing bowl so it resembles a pile of dirt)
1 package gummy worms
1 can chocolate icing
1 small package of red hots candy

Directions
After the devil's food cake is cool, apply icing liberally. After icing, sprinkle red hots on the cake and poke holes in it with your finger or a wooden spoon handle then insert the gummy worms so they sort of hang out. Serve with a great big Max Smile.

RUBY'S ANGEL FOOD CAKE WITH PINK ICING, BUTTERCREAM ROSES, SUGAR HEARTS, AND SPARKLY STARS

from *Bunny Cakes* by
Rosemary Wells, Dial:
ISBN 0803721439 (hc),
Puffin: 0140566678 (pbk).

■ Ruby is determined to make *her* kind of cake for her grandmother. In the book, Ruby's angel food cake is a bit lopsided, so you may want to kind of sit on the cake before you ice it, but it's going to make it look weird.

Ingredients
1 ready-made angel food cake
1 can pink icing
ready-made cake decorating flowers (available at groceries and Michael's craft stores)
sugar hearts (red hots candy) or gummy hearts

Directions
Buy a ready-made angel food cake and cover it with pink icing. You can usually buy cake decorating flowers in the bakery section of the grocery store to decorate. Sugar hearts are usually a bit harder to find if it isn't February, but you can always substitute gummy hearts.

BUTTERFLY SANDWICHES

to go with *The Butterfly Alphabet* by Kjell Block Sandved, Scholastic: ISBN 0590480030 (hc); *Butterfly House* by Eve Bunting, Scholastic: ISBN 0590848844 (hc); or *The Very Hungry Caterpillar* by Eric Carle, Putnam: ISBN 0399208534 (hc), Philomel: ISBN 0399226907 (board book).

■ The only thing better than watching butterflies is eating them. You can decorate these to look as real or imaginary as you like.

Ingredients

28 slices of butter-top bread (the top is shaped like half a heart)
butter
12 American process cheese slices
Cheez Doodles® (cheese-flavored corn curls)
licorice strings
mustard
ketchup
olive slices
pickle slices

Directions

Use butter-top bread because of its distinctive shape. Butter one side of each piece of bread. Put buttered side down in a hot griddle pan and lay one slice American Process cheese on bread, cover with another piece of bread, with the buttered side on the outside. Cook until nice and brown, crispy even. You need two sandwiches to make each butterfly. The rounded tops are the outside edges of the butterfly wings. Cut away about 1 inch from the bottom sides to make the "wings" wedge-shaped. Place a Cheez Doodle in between the two "wings," to be the body of the butterfly. Add two antennae made of licorice strings with a knot tied at the end. Decorate the butterfly wings with mustard and ketchup designs, and olive and pickle slices, and enjoy!

MONKEY BREAD to go

with *Caps for Sale* by Esphyr Slobodkina, HarperCollins: ISBN 020109147X (hc), HarperTrophy: 0064431436 (pbk).

■ The monkeys in the tree would love snatching pieces of this bread just the way they snatch the sleeping peddler's caps.

Ingredients

two cans Pillsbury Grands!® refrigerated biscuits (16 total)
1 stick butter
cinnamon
sugar

Directions

Cut biscuits in quarters. Dip pieces in melted butter then toss in cinnamon and sugar. Put into pie pan in a jumbled sort of arrangement, the ways monkeys would do it, and bake for 15 minutes at 350°F or until top browns. Serve to eager little readers after they've thoroughly acted out the story, with you being the peddler, carrying your imaginary caps for sale to town and sleeping against your imaginary tree while those bad monkeys steal your imaginary wares. Students will enjoy these NON-imaginary pieces of monkey bread.

EEL PIE to go with
Catherine Called Birdy by
Karen Cushman,
Houghton Mifflin: ISBN
0395681863 (hc),
HarperTrophy
0064405842 (pbk)

■ Catherine constantly complains about having to eat eel pie, among her other problems. Eel were kept in the moats of most castles as an easy source of protein that could survive the winter freezes. You're not likely to find eel in the supermarket so substitute scallops (about $10/lb), fake crabmeat ($3/lb), or pieces of white fish.

Ingredients
2 cups sesame seeds
1 teaspoon salt
1 teaspoon pepper
1 cup Hidden Valley Ranch® Dressing
1/2 pound scallops

Directions
Toast the sesame seeds until lightly browned on a cookie sheet (usually 300°F will do this in about 10 minutes. Let the seeds cool, and then mix salt and pepper into them. Pour the salad dressing into a bowl, then plop in the "eel" pieces (scallops). You actually could use real eel, if you could find it, but it's a pain to kill it and skin it, not to mention the bones. Take the easy way out. Trust me—it's much easier with scallops. Coat them well with the Hidden Valley dressing, then roll them in the sesame seeds until they're well coated. Spread the "eels" in a pie pan, cover with a ready-made pie crust, and make a hole in the crust. Bake at 450°F or until the eel is "stiff" when you poke it through the hole you cleverly made in the crust so the aroma of baking eels would waft through the classroom making all the kids gag and retch. It actually tastes pretty good, but if they think it's really eel, you're going to have a real battle trying to get them to eat it.

MEXICAN CRAB ROLL-UPS

to go with *Chadwick the Crab* by Priscilla Cummings, illustrated by A. R. Cohen, Tidewater Publishing: ISBN 087033347X (hc), *Crab Moon* by Ruth Horowitz, illustrated by Kate Kiesler, Candlewick: ISBN 0763607096; or *Follow Me* by Nancy Tafuri, Greenwillow: ISBN 0688087736 (hc).

■ In the *Chadwick* books, Chesapeake crabs have adventures of all sorts, and some end up as meals. *Crab Moon* is about the horseshoe crabs that these snack roll-ups sort of resemble. In *Follow Me*, a sea lion trails a wandering crab and comes upon a huge colony of crabs.

Ingredients
12 flour tortillas
2 cans ready-made bean dip (near potato chips in the grocery store)
shredded Monterey Jack cheese
2 cans crabmeat, drained

Other
paper plates

Directions
On a flour tortilla, spread about two tablespoons bean dip and sprinkle with a handful of shredded cheese. Add about one tablespoon of drained crabmeat. Nuke for 30 seconds. Fold in half, nuke for 30 seconds more. Let it cool before you eat it. Contributed by Chris Cole, computer doctor extraordinaire.

CHERRY COBBLER to go

with *Cherries and Cherry Pits* by Vera Williams, Greenwillow: ISBN 0688051456 (hc), Mulberry Books: 0688104789.

■ If you love cherries, you'll love this recipe.

Ingredients
2 cans of honey-butter-flavored flaky buttermilk biscuits, pulled apart into "leaves"
2 cans of prepared cherry pie filling mix

Directions
Place a layer of the biscuit "leaves" in the bottom of buttered heat-resistant glass custard dishes. Add a layer of pie filling. Add another layer of "leaves" and another layer of pie filling. End with a layer of biscuit leaves. Sprinkle with granulated sugar. Bake at 350°F for about an hour, until top layer of biscuits are browned. Serve with vanilla ice cream on top of the warm cobbler.

PALM TREES to go with *Chicka Chicka Boom Boom* by Bill Martin, Jr., and John Archambault, illustrated by Lois Ehlert, Simon & Schuster: ISBN 067167949X (hc).

■ In the story, critters go up and down a palm tree in search of the alphabet. You can make an edible version of the palm tree and surround it with alphabet cookies and critter cookies. The tree itself, while edible, is more for show.

Ingredients
1 cucumber
shredded coconut
raisins
alphabet cookies (Mothers brand or Costco gallon containers)
Healthy Advantage Ginger Animal Cookies

Other
toothpicks

Directions
Peel a skinny cucumber, and cut off the ends so it will stand up. At the top, using the peels you cut off, make palm-tree style leaves with scissors, then make it look like a palm tree by anchoring the pieces with a toothpick in the top of the "tree." Make a little island around the base of the "tree" with shredded coconut. Add raisins to look like little "coconuts." Add some alphabet cookies and Healthy Advantage Ginger Animal Cookies, and munch your way through the story.

FOXY LOXY'S FAVORITE CASEROLE to go with
Chicken Little by Steven Kellogg, William Morrow: ISBN 0688070450 (pbk).

■ This simple chicken casserole spells the end of unwitting hysterical chickens worldwide, so the world really *is* coming to an end it seems.

Ingredients
one bag of potato chips
2 precooked boneless chicken breasts cut up into little cubes or
1 large can of canned chicken
1/2 cup slivered almonds (these are "beaks")
1/2 teaspoon onion flakes
1/2 teaspoon salt
1 small jar drained pimentos (these are the cockscombs)
1 can cream of chicken soup
1/2 cup mayonnaise

Directions
The first step is to crush the potato chips. If you were Chicken Little, this would be done with pieces of falling sky as well as hysterical running around. Then spread the crushed potato chips in the bottom of a 9x14-inch baking dish (you could also make individual casseroles in heat-resistant glass custard cups). Mix all other ingredients in a large bowl. Pour over the crushed potato chips. Bake at 350°F for 30 minutes.

OVIPAROUS COOKIES

to go with *Chickens Aren't the Only Ones* by Ruth Heller, Price Stern Sloan: ISBN 0448018721 (hc).

■ After reading the story, students will know the word *oviparous* and will enjoy sharing these multisyllabic cookies with their friends.

Ingredients

1 cup butter
1 cup sugar
1 egg
5 hard-cooked, chopped
  eggs yolks

1 tablespoon grated lemon peel
3 cups flour
cookie-decorating sugar sprinkles

Other

round cookie cutter

Directions

Cream together butter, sugar, and raw egg. Add chopped hard-cooked egg yolks and lemon peel. Stir together well. To make dough, gradually add flour. Reserve a little bit for rolling the dough out. Roll dough one-finger thick using rolling pin, or pat the dough out with floured hands. Cut cookies with egg-shaped cookie cutters, or use circles and reshape cookies to look more like eggs. Bake on ungreased pan at 350°F for about 17 minutes. Decorate with sparkly sugar to make jeweled eggs.

GOOD BLOOD-SUCKING FUN to go with

The Chizzywink and the Alamagoozlum by Tony Johnston, illustrated by Robert Bender, Holiday House: 0823413594 (hc).

■ The mosquito's proboscis laps up its victim's sweet blood. Kids will love this little gory storytime snack.

Ingredients

maple syrup

Other

12 little ketchup containers from a fast-food place
12 coffee stirrers (they have to be hollow)

Directions

Fill each little container half-full with maple syrup and let the kids be mosquitoes and drink it up with teeny-tiny coffee stirrer straws, as if they were little mosquitoes lapping up blood.

KILLER MOUSSE

to go with *A Chocolate Moose for Dinner* by Fred Gwynne, Simon & Schuster: ISBN 0671666851 (hc).

■ Too often kids get the "moose" puns but have never tasted chocolate mousse. This is not complicated, but tastes like mousse. Remind them it's not hair mousse (we hope).

Ingredients
1 can sweetened condensed Eagle brand milk
2/3 cup Hershey's chocolate syrup
2 cups whipping cream (or 1 container Cool Whip®)

Directions
In a large bowl, stir together milk and chocolate syrup. Fold in whipped cream. Pour into waffle cups (found near the ice cream cones and chocolate syrup usually). Freeze these little mousses until solid. Let them thaw for about five minutes before eating.

I CAN'T BELIEVE I DANCED AWAY THE NIGHT CHILI

to go with any version of *Cinderella*, but for an interesting new twist, check out *Cindy Ellen: A Wild West Cinderella* by Susan Lowell, illustrations by Jane K. Manning, HarperCollins: ISBN 0060274468 (hc).

■ Lowell's buckaroo version of the classic tale calls for a Tex-Mex chili treat. You could eat it out of a bowl, or serve it traditionally on a piece of cornbread

Ingredients
1 package precooked bratwurst cut into "coins"
1 onion, chopped
1/2 pound bacon, crumbled
1 can crushed tomatoes
1 tablespoon sugar
1 teaspoon yellow mustard (prepared)
1 can pinto beans
1 can kidney beans
1 can garbanzo beans
1 can navy beans

Directions
Put everything into a crock-pot and cook on low overnight while you dance and party. In one version of the *Cinderella* story, her evil stepmother tells her she can go to the ball if she can separate out the beans, and she dumps a bag of beans of each kind into the courtyard. Cinderella gets her friends, the birds, to extract them for her.

EMILY ELIZABETH BISCUITS to go with

Clifford the Big Red Dog by Norman Bridwell, Scholastic: ISBN 0590407430 (hc), 059044297X (pbk).

■ These dog biscuits are tasty for little girls, big dogs, and just about everyone.

Ingredients
1 cup peanut butter
1 cup dry milk
2 tablespoons honey
graham cracker crumbs

Other
dog biscuit-shaped cookie cutter

Directions
Moosh together peanut butter, dry milk, and honey. Roll or pat dough out on a bed of graham cracker crumbs and cut out with cookie cutter. Flop over so crumbs coat the other side too. Let it set until snack time.

CLOUDY WITH A CHANCE OF MEATBALLS

to go with the book *Cloudy with a Chance of Meatballs* by Judi Barrett, illustrated by Ron Barrett, Simon & Schuster: ISBN 0689707495 (pbk), 0689306474 (lb).

■ In the town of ChewandSwallow, you better hope you don't get whacked on the head by one of these substantial meatballs.

Ingredients
2 pounds ground round
1 cup seasoned bread crumbs
1 package dry onion soup mix
3 eggs

Directions
Moosh all the ingredients together by hand in a large bowl. Form into walnut size meatballs. Nuke for 10 minutes at 50% (preferably on a microwave bacon platter if you have one). If you want to avoid a mess in the microwave, cover with a couple of paper towels. Spoon out excess melted fat while the platter is still in the Nukemaster microwave. If you like the smell of browning meatballs, you could alternatively use an electric skillet to cook the meatballs. When they are done cooking, remove meatballs to a plate so they don't roll off and escape across the floor.

MARSHMALLOW SPIDERS to go with

Cobweb Christmas by Shirley Climo, illustrated by Joe Lasker, HarperTrophy: ISBN 006443110X (pbk)

■ The spiders decorate the old woman's Christmas tree for her, then kind of hang around to celebrate with her. These could also be enjoyed with other books about spiders.

Ingredients

12 large marshmallows
sunflower kernels
lots of string licorice (the kind that's like spaghetti)

Directions

Use the marshmallow to make the "body" of the spider. Poke the sunflower kernel eyes right into the marshmallow. Then poke holes in the marshmallow with a toothpick to anchor the legs made from pieces of string licorice. There's nothing worse than having the spider's legs fall off before you eat them!

SILLY OLD BEAR'S COTTLESTON PIE to go

with *The Complete Poems of Winnie-the-Pooh* by A. A. Milne, illustrated by Ernest H. Shepard: ISBN 0525460772 (hc).

■ Pooh's refrain about Cottleston Pie always puzzles kids since they haven't got a clue what it is!

Ingredients

2 prebaked, 9-inch pie shells
1 cup bite-sized pieces of ham or bacon
6 eggs
4 cups whipping cream
1 teaspoon salt
1/2 teaspoon nutmeg
4 tablespoons butter
1 cup grated cheese

Directions

Put half of the bacon/ham and cheese on the bottom of the pie shell. Beat eggs and whipping cream with salt and nutmeg in a bowl. Pour on top of bacon/ham and cheese. Sprinkle remaining cheese and bacon/ham and dot with butter. Set on middle rack of oven and bake about 30 minutes at 350°F until puffed and brown. Let stand 10 minutes before cutting. You could also make individual "pies" in heat-resistant glass custard cups. You can nuke this, but use 50% power or the eggs turn to rubber.

HICKORY DICKORY DOCK CLOCKS to go

with *The Completed Hickory Dickory Dock* by Jim Aylesworth, illustrated by Eileen Christelow, Aladdin: ISBN 0689718624 (pbk).

■ Each hungry youngster can make a clock and mouse and later snack on it, thus giving new meaning to "having a good time."

Ingredients
1 cucumber sliced into rounds
10 baby carrots
12 graham crackers
12 cheese sticks
12 gray jellybeans

Directions
Build this project on a paper plate. Use an unpeeled cucumber slice for each clock face. Add carrot slivers for the clock hands. A graham cracker is the clock body and a piece of string cheese is the pendulum. Add a gray jellybean for the mouse.

BANANA BOAT SNACKS

to go with *Counting Crocodiles* by Judy Sierra, illustrated by Will Hillenbrand, Harcourt Brace: ISBN 015200191 (hc).

■ Getting across a sea filled with crocodiles is easier for little monkeys who like bananas made into boats.

Ingredients
12 bananas
1 jar marshmallow fluff
1 container "squirt" jelly
sunflower seed kernels
12 Healthy Advantage Ginger Animal cookies (monkeys)

Directions
Cut 12 bananas in half lengthwise on 12 paper plates. Spread each banana half with a layer of marshmallow fluff. Add a thin layer of squirt jelly. Reassemble the banana halves and add sunflower kernel "eyes." Perch one monkey on top of each banana crocodile before you eat them all.

EASY POSOLE to go with
*The Day It Snowed
Tortillas* by Joe Hayes,
Illustrated by
Lucy Jelinek, Mariposa
Publishing: ISBN
0933553005 (pbk).

■ A clever housewife outwits thieves with tortillas all over the lawn one morning. This is a traditional winter dish served with flour tortillas.

Ingredients
2 cans chicken broth
1 frozen container chopped green chili
2 potatoes cut into cubes
2 tablespoons onion flakes
2 tablespoons garlic flakes
1 teaspoon dried or fresh cilantro
1 6-ounce can chicken
1 can hominy, drained

Directions
Combine all ingredients in a crock-pot. Let it bubble away for a couple of hours. To serve, ladle into cups or bowls, and let each child tear up fresh flour tortillas into little bite-sized pieces to put into the posole. Eat with a spoon.

**BOA CONSTRICTOR
BREADSTICKS** to go with
*The Day Jimmy's Boa Ate
the Wash* by Trinka Hakes
Noble, illustrated by
Steven Kellogg, Dial
Press: ISBN 0803717237;
also good with *Verdi*
by Janelle Cannon.

■ Instead of hanging around in the trees or in the laundry, these breadstick snakes can hang around the students for a while before they get eaten.

Ingredients
2 packages refrigerated breadstick dough (eight per can)
green and yellow cake-decorating sprinkles
3 eggs, beaten
silver cake-decorating beads or sprinkles for eyes

Other
a brush for brushing the snakes

Directions
Each breadstick becomes a little boa constrictor when kids pat on yellow and green spots of decorating sugar after "painting" the snakes with egg so the sugar sticks. After the bread dough sticks look "snaky" enough, add silver bullet eyes. Put on cookie sheet in the shape you want them. Bake at 350°F about seven minutes.

THE DAY MY DOGS BECAME GUYS FEAST

to go with *The Day My Dogs Became Guys* by Merrill Markoe, illustrated by Eric Brace, Viking: ISBN 0670853445 (hc).

■ When out-of-control dogs turn into guys they have a feast with all the food that was in the refrigerator for the family party that evening.

Ingredients

1/2 pound sliced turkey breast
1/2 pound sliced roast beef
1 package cheddar cheese slices
1 package chocolate chip cookies

Directions

Cut the turkey, roast beef, and cheese into quarters. Build the meat and cheese into "sandwiches" between two chocolate chip cookies. It really tastes quite unique. Dogs will love them and so will kids.

DINOSAUR PIZZA to go

with *Dinosaur Pizza* by Lee Wardlaw, illustrated by Julie Durrell, Troll: ISBN 0816744343 (pbk).

■ When Jill's best friend moves away, she's left all alone until Bobbi Jo asks her to join the Lunch Bunch Club, a wacky group of kids who bring unusual snacks and lunches to school every day. Will Jill's Dinosaur Pizza be "tyrannorific" enough to keep her in the club, or will she learn that it takes more than "dino-mite" food to make a true friend?

Ingredients

1 jar Pizza Quick® sauce
12 small ready-made Boboli pizza shells (they come two to a package)
1 package grated mozzarella cheese
24 whole black olives, drained
24 whole green olives, drained
24 pepperoni slices
1 green bell pepper cut into small triangles to look like fangs

Directions

Preheat oven to 450°F. Spoon a layer of pizza sauce onto each pizza shell. Sprinkle mozzarella cheese on top of the sauce on each shell. To make a dinosaur face, use two black olives for eyes, two green olives for nostrils, pepperoni slices for rosy cheeks. Arrange the pepper "fangs" to look like the dinosaur's mouth is open. Place the pizzas on a cookie sheet and bake for eight to 10 minutes until the cheese bubbles and begins to brown. Remove from oven and cool a few minutes before slicing. You can experiment with zucchini, mushrooms, onion slices, pineapple, cooked chicken, meatballs, and canned corn kernels too. Contributed by Lee Wardlaw.

COCONUT TREAT to go

with *Doctor Bird: Three Lookin' Up Tales from Jamaica* by Gerald Hausman, illustrated by Ashley Wolff, Putnam/Penguin: ISBN 039922744X (hc).

■ Doctor Bird shows Mouse how to survive after a Jamaican hurricane. Mouse is told to "look up, not down." After climbing the coconut tree is told, "If you can get through the hard, you can sip through the soft." Mouse chews a hole in the coconut and uses his tail to dip into the nut. By licking his tail dry, he gets lots of the sweet coconut milk, then eats the white meat and fills his belly.

Ingredients	Other
2 coconuts	hammer for cracking
brown sugar	knives for prying out coconut meat

Directions

Take two very hard brown coconuts. With adult help, put a hole in each so you can drain the clear water, or milk, inside. Reserve this for a refreshing drink. Then crack the coconut and using a butter knife, pry the white "meat" off the hard shell. Put these pieces of coconut meat on a plate, then sprinkle brown sugar on top (not too much) and let it sit for about 10 minutes while you drink your coconut juice. The brown sugar should soak into the nut meat a bit and make it very tasty. Contributed by the author.

DOGZILLA BARBECUE to

go with *Dogzilla* by Dav Pilkey, Harcourt Brace: ISBN 0152239448 (hc), 0152239456 (pbk).

■ The evil Dogzilla is lured to his doom by this irresistible barbecue.

Ingredients

2 pounds lean ground beef
2 cups barbecue sauce
1 grated onion (you can reduce this if your students hate onions)
1 package grated cheddar cheese
2 cans refrigerated biscuits

Directions

Stir together the beef, barbecue sauce, and onion. Moosh it all together with your fingers, or your paws if you are Dogzilla today. Press a biscuit into each cup of a muffin tin, pressing out the dough all the way to the top of the cup. Fill each cup with a glob of the barbecue stuff and sprinkle on cheddar cheese. Bake at 400°F about 15 minutes, until the meat is cooked through.

LIVER LOVER TREAT to go with *Don't Forget the Bacon!* by Pat Hutchins, Mulberry Books: ISBN 0688087434 (pbk).

■ Children seldom willingly eat liver, but they may taste this and like it because of the bacon—which you cannot forget.

Ingredients
1 pint chicken livers
1 package thin-sliced bacon
1 can water chestnuts (optional)

Other
toothpicks

Directions
Wrap the bacon around the chicken liver piece and pin it in place with a toothpick. Alternatively you can tuck the piece of water chestnut into each "package" of chicken liver wrapped in bacon with your finger (it really feels gross). Put bacon/liver bundles on a baking sheet. Bake at 350°F for about 40 minutes, until the bacon is crispy and brown. Remind the kids to take the toothpick out before they eat the liver treats. That's assuming you can get them to eat it.

MRS. MCDOOL'S FLUFFY BISCUITS from *The Dream Stealer* by Stephen Cosgrove, illustrated by Carol Heyer, Graphic Arts: ISBN 1558680098 (pbk).

■ Mrs. McDool is standing at a cutting board making a lunch of sausages and biscuits for the characters to take on their journey. The model used for Mrs. McDool was Merilyn Heyer, the illustrator's mother, and this is her recipe for fluffy biscuits.

Ingredients

1 cup flour
1 teaspoon baking powder
1/8 teaspoon baking soda
1/4 teaspoon salt

2 tablespoons unsalted butter
1/4 cup plus 1 teaspoon of heavy cream

Directions

Preheat oven to 375°F. Sift and combine the dry ingredients in a bowl. Cut in the butter until the mixture resembles pea-sized crumbs. Add the cream a little at a time and mix with a spoon until all of the ingredients are combined and form a ball of dough. Don't overwork or over handle the dough or it will become tough. Lightly flour a cutting board and roll out the dough to about a 1/2-inch thickness. Using a round cutter, press out the biscuits and place the dough rounds on wax paper or a parchment-lined baking sheet. You can roll the leftover dough again to make more biscuits, but the texture of these will be denser than the others. Bake until golden on the top and brown on the bottom, about 15 minutes. These fluffy biscuits are best served warm with sweet butter and honey, and of course plump sausages, which are featured prominently in the story. Contributed by Carol Heyer.

CANNONBALL STEW to go with *Drummer Hoff* by Barbara Emberly, illustrated by Ed Emberly, Simon & Schuster: ISBN 0671662481 (hc), Aladdin: 067166249X (pbk).

■ If you could shoot meatballs out of Drummer Hoff's cannon, they'd look like these cannonballs.

Ingredients

2 pounds ground turkey
1 cup bread crumbs
1 teaspoon onion salt

1 cup grated carrot
1 cup grated zucchini
poppy seeds

Directions

Moosh everything together and make into 12 cannonball-sized meatballs. Roll each meatball thoroughly in poppy seeds to make it gray as a cannonball. Bake on a cookie sheet at 350°F an hour. To serve, you could stack them up like cannonballs and let the kids pick them up with fingers.

QUALITY TIME BABY BUNNY SNACK to go

with *The Dumb Bunnies*
by Sue Denim, illustrated
by Dav Pilkey, Scholastic:
ISBN 0590477080 (hc).

■ This snack is found in one of the pictures in this first story of the Dumb Bunnies. You can make the little flags out of paper triangles wrapped around toothpicks.

Ingredients
1 can creamed corn
12 premade yellow cupcakes

Other
12 little flags on toothpicks (flags should read, "Hooray")

Directions
Dig a little hole out of the center of each cupcake. Put a tablespoon of creamed corn in the hole. Nuke for two minutes. After these cool about two minutes, insert little hooray flags and eat. The juice from the creamed corn kind of melts into the cupcake, making it soggy but not mooshy, just the way a Dumb Bunny would love it.

SPAM HULA DELIGHT

to go with *The Dumb Bunnies* by Sue Denim, illustrated by Dav Pilkey, Scholastic: ISBN 0590477080 (hc).

■ If the Dumb Bunnies ever make it to Hawaii, they'll likely discover how to make this island favorite.

Ingredients
1/4 cup soy sauce
1/4 cup sugar
1/4 cup 7 UP
1 teaspoon ground ginger
1 can SPAM® canned luncheon meat

Directions
In a saucepan, mix together soy sauce, sugar, 7 UP, and ginger and bring to a boil. Cut SPAM into little cubes, and add to sauce. Cook about five minutes, until luncheon meat is warmed. Eat with toothpicks.

DUMB BUNNIES EASTER EGGS to go with *The Dumb Bunnies Easter* by Sue Denim, illustrated by Dav Pilkey, Scholastic: ISBN 0590202413 (hc), 0590202421 (pbk).

■ Of course, the Dumb Bunnies can't be expected to make "normal" Easter eggs because they don't do anything the normal way. These are certainly NOT normal eggs.

Ingredients
1 jar peanut butter
1 box confectioners' sugar
1 bag semisweet chocolate chips
1 small block paraffin (canning wax)

Other
wooden skewers
heat-resistant glass dish

Directions
Wash your hands (unless you're a Dumb Bunny). Put peanut butter into a large bowl. Add a cup of sugar and moosh it into the peanut butter. Continue to moosh as much sugar into the peanut butter as possible with your hands. The heat of your hands helps in the mooshing process. When the mixture is the consistency of play dough, make little Easter egg shapes the size of your little toe and place on wax paper. Melt the chocolate chips and paraffin in the heat-resistant dish in the Nukemaster microwave. Skewer each Easter egg and dip into the melted chocolate coating mix. Let the excess chocolate drip off over the bowl. Unskewer the eggs onto wax paper and let the coating set.

BLACK AND WHITE SNACK to go with *Dylan's Day Out* by Peter Catalanotto, Orchard: ISBN 0531058298 (hc).

■ Dylan is a Dalmatian, and he loves only black and white stuff. For a snack, he would prefer goodies like this.

Ingredients
1 package Oreo® cookies
1 quart vanilla ice cream
1 container whipped cream or Cool Whip®

Directions
Open up Oreo cookies, spoon a small scoop of ice cream in the middle, and then close the cookie again, smooshing to make a "sandwich." Top each little snack with whipped cream or Cool whip.

LITTLE WATERSPOUT SPIDERS to go with *The Eensy-Weensy Spider* by Mary Ann Hoberman, illustrated by Nadine Westcott, Little Brown: ISBN 031636338 (hc).

■ These eensy-weensy spiders come sliding out of the waterspout into the paper cup, ready to eat. We tried it with miniature marshmallows too, and they got rather gooey and sticky, not nearly as appealing as these little guys.

Ingredients
green grapes
shoestring licorice but into 2-inch pieces
miniature chocolate chips
1 gallon Kool-Aid® or lemonade

Other
aluminum foil
paper cups

Directions
Take a green grape and carefully poke four holes through the grape with a skewer or toothpick for the legs made of pieces of shoestring licorice. Insert legs into holes in sides of grape so they stick out the other side. Carefully poke two holes for the "eyes," and insert a tiny chocolate chip in each hole. Serve these little green spiders in "waterspouts" made of aluminum foil shaped into tubes. You can "wash the spider out" with Kool-Aid poured through the waterspout into a paper cup, and after the kids drink the liquid they can eat the spiders. Since this snack takes a lot of effort for one very tiny snack, you might want to have kids make more than one spider and also read other books about spiders.

OVIPAROUS SAILBOATS to go with *Egg Thoughts and Other Frances Songs* by Russell Hoban, HarperCollins: ISBN 0064433781 (hc).

■ Frances hates eggs of every kind, but she might have tasted these little sailboats.

Ingredients
12 hard-boiled eggs
12 processed cheese slices

Other
12 wooden skewers

Directions
The first part of the fun is teaching kids how to peel an egg so it doesn't look like a scary science project. Show them how to crack the shell on a hard surface then pry off the pieces and peel off the membrane. Cut the egg in half. Cut each cheese slice in half diagonally, so it's a triangle. Break each skewer in half. (You could also teach a mini-lesson on "halves" with this snack) Carefully spear the cheese slice with the skewer so it looks like a sail on a mast. Insert skewer into egg "boats." When you eat them, remind kids not to eat the skewers.

ROCK CAKES to go with *Elizabeti's Doll* by Stephanie Stuve-Bodeen, illustrated by Christy Hale, Lee and Low: ISBN 1880000709 (hc).

■ The story is about a Tanzanian girl who has a rock for a doll. The entry originated from a recipe collected by the author when she lived in Tanzania.

Ingredients

2 cups flour
2 teaspoons baking powder
1/2 teaspoon nutmeg
1/2 teaspoon cinnamon
1/4 teaspoon ground cloves
1/4 cup cold butter
1/4 cup vegetable shortening (Crisco®)

1/3 cup raisins
1/3 cup walnuts
2/3 cup light brown sugar
grated lemon peel of 1 lemon
1 egg
milk

Directions

Sift together flour, baking powder, nutmeg, cinnamon, and cloves. With your fingers, mash in cold butter and vegetable shortening until mixture is crumbly. Stir in raisins, walnuts, and light brown sugar. Add lemon peel, egg, and just enough milk to make the dough stiff. Drop heaping tablespoons of the dough about 2 inches apart on a greased baking sheet, and bake in a preheated 400°F oven until golden, about 12-15 minutes. Serve fresh—they're hard as rocks the next day. Contributed by the author.

FARMER DUCK'S BILLS to go with *Farmer Duck* by Martin Waddell, illustrated by Helen Oxenbury, Candlewick Press, 1564020096 (hc).

■ The animals get tired of doing all the work. If only they could send the farmer an itemized bill—or a "duck bill."

Ingredients

12 dried apricots
melted chocolate chips
chocolate chips (tiny)

Directions

Dip the ugliest end of each dried apricot into chocolate chips that have been melted in the microwave, and wave the dried fruit around until the chocolate hardens. Put two little, teeny-tiny chocolate pieces to look like the "nostrils" on the uncovered end of the "duck bill." Let the chocolate harden before you eat them.

FORGOTTEN SNOWFLAKES from
Christmas Is Coming by Charles and Debra Ghigna, illustrated by Mary O'Keefe, Charlesbridge: ISBN

■ Enjoy these edible wintry snowflakes that resemble Father Goose's winter treat.

Ingredients
2 egg whites
1/8 teaspoon cream of tartar
1/8 teaspoon salt
2/3 cup sugar
1 teaspoon vanilla extract
1 cup semisweet chocolate chips

Directions
Preheat oven to 375°F, and lightly grease a cookie sheet. In small mixer bowl, beat egg whites with cream of tartar and salt until soft peaks form. Gradually add sugar, beating until stiff peaks form. Carefully fold in vanilla extract and chocolate chips. Drop by teaspoonfuls onto prepared cookie sheet. Place cookie sheet into preheated oven. Immediately turn off oven and allow cookies to remain in oven six hours or overnight without opening door. Remove cookies from cookie sheet. Store in airtight container in cool dry place. Makes about 30 cookies. Contributed by the authors.

FLOWER FACE SANDWICHES to go with
The Flower Garden by Eve Bunting, illustrated by Kathryn Hewitt, Voyager: ISBN 0152023720 (hc).

■ The garden's delights can be artistically matched in these open-face treats.

Ingredients
white bread	basil
cream cheese	olives
cucumbers	pimentos
chive stems	

Directions
Cut a piece of white bread into a diamond shape and cover with cream cheese. Make a flower head from a cucumber slice that has been gouged down the sides to make indentations for the petals. A stem of a piece of chive has leaves added to it made of basil. For the center of the flower, use a piece of olive or pimento.

FOREST CHILD'S GRANOLA to go with

Forest Child by Marni McGee, illustrated by A. Scott Banfill, Green Tiger/Simon & Schuster: ISBN 0671866087 (hc), Aladdin/Simon & Schuster: 0689825781 (pbk).

■ When a child wanders into the forest and becomes lost, the animals say they do not help because "humans come only to catch and kill us." After the child rescues a rabbit caught in a trap, the creatures take turns playing with him, feeding him, and tucking him in for the night on a mat woven from flowers and bits of grass, and with a pillow made from moss. For the boy's dinner, the bear offers to "share the ripe, red berries that grow on prickly vines and the honey hidden in the hollows of trees." Not to be outdone, the squirrel promises to show the child "where to find some seeds, sweet and good to eat." These ingredients form the basis for a tasty and easy-to-make granola or trail mix.

Ingredients
1/2 cup pumpkin seed kernels
1 1/2 cups raw, chopped almonds
3 cups old-fashioned rolled oats
1/2 cup sunflower seeds
1/2 cup sesame seeds
1/2 cup coconut
1/2 cup powdered milk
3/4 teaspoon salt
1 teaspoon cinnamon
1/2 cups dried cranberries
1/2 cup raisins

In a small saucepan, heat:
1/2 cup honey
1/4 cup pure maple syrup
1/2 cup butter

Directions
Preheat oven to 325°F. To make the granola, combine the dry ingredients in a large bowl. Pour the honey mixture over the dry ingredients and toss until well coated. Spray two flat baking sheets with vegetable oil spray and spread the mixture out on them. After baking 15 minutes, turn the granola over a bit with a spatula and continue baking for 10-15 minutes. It will be golden and fragrant when done. When cooled, store in an airtight container. Contributed by the author.

FROGS AND TOADS IN HOLES to go with *Frog and Toad Treasury* by Arnold Lobel, HarperCollins: ISBN 0060267887 (hc).

■ This traditional breakfast treat can go with any *Frog and Toad* book. Nobody seems too certain why they're called "Toad in the Hole" in Britain. Perhaps because they have that one eggy "eye" looking up at you when they're cooked?

Ingredients
1 pound thin-sliced bacon
1 dozen large or jumbo eggs

Directions
Line each cup of a metal muffin tin with a piece of bacon around the sides and a mosaic of little bacon pieces across the bottom. Without breaking the yolk, slide a raw egg into each cup. Bake at 350°F until the bacon is done and the eggs are cooked all the way through, about 30 minutes. If you can find metal cupcake papers, it makes the cleanup considerably easier.

GEORGE AND MARTHA'S FAVORITE SPLIT PEA SOUP to go with *George and Martha* by James Marshall, Houghton Mifflin: ISBN 0395166195 (hc), 0395199727 (pbk).

■ Martha loves to make split pea soup, but George hates to eat it. When they finally get honest about it, they eat chocolate chip cookies instead because "friends don't make friends eat split pea soup."

Ingredients
2 packages of refrigerated chocolate chip cookie dough

Directions
Slice cookie dough about as thick as a finger. Put six cookies on a microwavable plate, equally spaced. Nuke each batch of six cookies about a minute, until they puff up and then collapse. Let them cool before you eat them, or you'll be sorry!

JAN BRETT'S GINGERBREAD BABY to
go with *The Gingerbread Baby* by Jan Brett, Putnam: ISBN 0399234446 (hc). For directions on putting together gingerbread houses, look at *Gingerbread Houses: Baking and Building Memories* by Nonnie Cargas, Krause Publications: ISBN 0873417119 (pbk).

■ This version of the traditional tale ends with the runaway Gingerbread Baby being lured back to the safety of a gingerbread house.

Ingredients
1 cup butter
1 cup sugar
2 teaspoons ground ginger
1/2 teaspoon ground cloves
2 teaspoons baking soda
4 cups flour
4 eggs
2 cups molasses
1 1/2 cups hot water
canned vanilla icing

Directions
Divide kids into six or seven groups. Each group is going to perform one major step in the production of gingerbread from scratch.

Group 1: In a bowl, cream together butter and sugar
Group 2: In a separate bowl, mix together ginger, cloves, baking soda, and flour
Group 3: Mix eggs into the butter batter
Group 4: Mix molasses into the butter batter
Group 5: Add hot water to the butter batter
Group 6: In a third bowl, combine one cup of the butter batter mixture and one of the cup dry ingredients together.
Group 7: Do the same as Group 6, and continue until all ingredients are mixed.

Pour into greased and floured baking sheets. Bake at 325°F for about 30 minutes or until a toothpick inserted in middle comes out clean. Let cool. When you use this to make gingerbread houses, you can use canned icing as the glue.

YUMMY GINGERBREAD BOYS to go with *The Gingerbread Boy* by Paul Galdone, Clarion: ISBN 0899191630 (pbk), 0395287995 (lb).

■ This recipe originally calls for a mouthful of water (to make the gingerbread rise), but you can use your discretion on how to add the water to the mixture. It works like Play-Doh® when you get it all mixed together, and no amount of excessive child handling will ruin it. It also doesn't stick to anything, so the cleanup is very easy.

Ingredients
1 package gingerbread mix
vegetable oil
water
icing out of a can
raisins
red hots

Other
gingerbread boy cookie cutter (optional)

Directions
Follow directions on package of gingerbread except use oil in the amount called for instead of water. Add about "a mouthful" (2 tablespoons) of water. Moosh it together with your hands or a wooden spoon. When it becomes a consistency like Play-Doh®, make gingerbread boys by hand or use a cookie cutter. To each cookie, add red hots for eyes and a raisin for a nose. Bake at 350°F for about ten minutes. When cool, add icing details.

REAL GINGERBREAD MEN to go with *The Gingerbread Man* by Jim Aylesworth, illustrated by Barbara McClintock, Scholastic: ISBN 0590972197 (pbk).

■ This traditional recipe comes right off the back of the book by the author's request. It's very old-fashioned.

Ingredients
2 1/2 cups flour
1 teaspoon baking powder
1/4 teaspoon baking soda
1/4 teaspoon salt
1 teaspoon ground cinnamon
1 teaspoon ground ginger
1 teaspoon ground cloves
1/4 teaspoon allspice
1 farm fresh egg
1 cup firmly packed dark brown sugar
2/3 cup dark molasses
6 tablespoons softened butter

Directions
Sift flour, baking powder, baking soda, salt, cinnamon, ginger, cloves, and allspice into a big bowl and mix together well. In another bowl, beat together egg, brown sugar, molasses, and butter. Add the dry ingredients to the wet ingredients until mixed well. Blend and refrigerate one hour. Roll out onto a floured board, cut with a floured gingerbread-man-shaped cookie cutter. Use raisins to decorate and place on a buttered cookie sheet. Bake at 350°F for eight minutes.

SAM-I-AM'S FEAST to go with *Green Eggs and Ham* by Dr. Seuss, Random House: ISBN 0394800168 (hc), 039400162 (lb).

■ Sam-I-Am says he won't eat them here, there, or anywhere, but in the end he does—and he likes green eggs and ham. Kids will like them, too, if they're made with this recipe

Ingredients
12 eggs
blue food coloring
1 can SPAM® canned luncheon meat, cut into 1/2-inch cubes

Other
12 small Pyrex® or other heat-resistant custard cups

Directions
If you're letting the kids crack the eggs, make sure they know that it's easier to get broken shells out of the bowl with a larger piece of a shell than with their fingers. Mix the eggs in a large bowl. Add one drop of blue food coloring for each egg. Divide SPAM cubes among the 12 custard cups. Pour egg mixture into the cups. Nuke for two minutes at 50%. Stir. Nuke some more (always at 50% or the eggs get all rubbery), until it gels up. It looks awful but tastes like regular eggs.

CRUDITÉS AND DIP to go
with *Gregory, the Terrible Eater* by Mitchell Sharmat, illustrated by Jose Aruego and Ariane Dewey, Simon & Schuster: ISBN

■ Gregory the goat just won't eat within the typical goat diet his parents want him to, preferring instead to eat "yucky" vegetables. This is your big chance to introduce the "fancy" term for cold, sliced veggies.

Ingredients
1 bottle ranch dressing
1 bunch celery cut into strips
12 carrots cut into strips
1 jicama cut into strips
several green, yellow, or red bell peppers cut into strips
1 zucchini cut into julienne strips
12 small paper cups

Directions
Slice all vegetables into 3-inch lengths and arrange artfully on a platter. Fill each paper cup with about 3 ounces of Ranch dressing "dip." Let students dip veggies into dip and eat—this way they are double-dipping in their own sauce.

QUICK STRAWBERRY JAM to go with *The Grey Lady and the Strawberry Snatcher* by Molly Bang, Aladdin: ISBN 0689803818 (pbk), Simon & Schuster: 0027081400 (lb), or *Strawberry Girl* by Lois Lenski, Lippincott: ISBN 039730109X (hc), 0397301103 (lb).

■ Strawberry stories give you a great excuse to make this unique easy jam.

Ingredients
2 to 3 cups mashed strawberries
3 cups sugar
1 package strawberry Jell-O®

Directions
Mix strawberries and sugar and let stand four hours or even overnight. Then in a saucepan, bring to a hard boil, then reduce heat to medium and boil 10 minutes. Remove from heat. Add Jell-O and mix until well dissolved. Bring to boiling point again. Remove from heat and let set a few minutes. Stir again. Put in jars and keep in refrigerator or freezer. Contributed by Phyllis Scholz.

YUMMY APHID SALAD

to go with *The Grouchy Ladybug* by Eric Carle, HarperCollins: ISBN 006027087X (pbk).

■ Aphids make up the traditional diet of ladybugs. Sesame seeds are a nice look-alike version for this snack.

Ingredients
12 peach halves
Smucker's Magic Shell chocolate topping
clean spinach leaves
sesame seeds
1 cup ranch salad dressing

Directions
Pour some of the salad dressing on a plate. Spread sesame seeds on another plate. Dip the bottom of the spinach leaves into the salad dressing and then dip the bottom side of the spinach leaf into sesame seeds. These are the aphids. Lay each "snack" on its own plate with a "grouchy" ladybug made from a peach half in the middle. Use Magic Shell topping to add chocolate spots and ladybug-like markings on the peach.

CROCK-POT SNACK to go

with *Growing Vegetable Soup* by Lois Ehlert, Harcourt Brace: ISBN 0152325751 (hc), 0152325808 (pbk).

■ All the ingredients for this yummy soup are mentioned in the book.

Ingredients
12 green onions, chopped
2 potatoes, chopped
4 carrots, sliced
1 stalk celery, sliced
12 green beans, cut into pieces
1 zucchini, quartered and sliced
1 can tomatoes
1 cup frozen peas
1 can chicken broth
1 can vegetable broth
1 teaspoon dried parsley
salt and pepper

Directions
Put everything into large crock-pot and cook for about three hours. Add salt and pepper to taste.

GUS AND GRANDPA'S CHRISTMAS COOKIES

from *Gus and Grandpa and the Christmas Cookies* by Claudia Mills, illustrated by Catherine Stock, Farrar, Straus, and Giroux: ISBN 0374328234 (hc).

■ As Gus and Grandpa are busy baking Christmas cookies, the doorbell keeps ringing, as all the neighbor ladies flood them with gifts of more cookies. They end up sharing their surplus cookies with a local homeless shelter. Children using this recipe can make their own cookies just like Gus and Grandpa's—to eat or to share!

Ingredients
1 cup granulated sugar
1/2 cup (one stick) butter or margarine
1 egg
3 tablespoons milk
1 teaspoon vanilla
2 cups flour
1 teaspoon baking powder
1/4 teaspoon salt

Other
cookie cutters

Directions
Cream together butter and sugar. Add eggs, milk, and vanilla. Beat well. Sift flour, baking powder, and salt. Add to butter mixture, beating until blended. Chill for at least two hours. Roll out dough to a 1/4-inch thickness. Cut with holiday cutters. Bake at 350°F for 10 minutes.

Frosting:
2 cups confectioners' sugar
1/3 cup milk or water
food coloring
colored sprinkles

Stir sugar and milk/water together until you get the desired consistency. Add a few drops of food coloring and stir some more. Spread on cookies and top with sprinkles. Contributed by Claudia Mills.

FAIRIES' FAVORITE TREAT to go with

Halloween: A Celtic Celebration by Grainne Rowland (available from the author by calling 334-660-1395).

■ On Halloween Night, the Irish people put out treats like these for the fairies to ensure good luck for the following year.

Ingredients

12 sugar ice cream cones
6 oranges
6 apples
6 bananas
1 pound seedless grapes

1 pound strawberries
chocolate syrup
1 cup chopped nuts
1 cup shredded coconut
milk for drinking

Directions

Dice and slice fruit into small pieces. Fill the sugar cone with the fruit pieces of your choice. Pour a little bit of chocolate syrup on top, then top with nuts and coconut. Drink a tall glass of milk with the treat. Contributed by the author.

LITTLE BEAR'S EDIBLE BIRTHDAY MOON HATS

to go with *Happy Birthday, Moon* by Frank Asch, Simon & Schuster: ISBN 0689835442 (pbk), 0689835434 (lb).

■ These little edible hats look like Little Bear's top hat that gets caught in a tree.

Ingredients

1 large Hershey Bar or 1 bag chocolate chips
12 marshmallows
12 chocolate wafer cookies

Other

12 wooden skewers
wax paper

Directions

Melt chocolate in microwavable bowl. Put a marshmallow on a skewer. Dip into chocolate and cover completely. Place chocolate-coated marshmallow on chocolate wafer on wax paper. Excess chocolate will run off the marshmallow to form brim of the hat and should adhere the marshmallow to the chocolate wafer. The chocolate should set in about five minutes.

RIP VAN WINKLE'S WAKE-UP OLYKOEKS

to go with *The Headless Horseman Rides Tonight* by Jack Prelutsky, illustrated by Arnold Lobel, Greenwillow: ISBN 0688117058 (pbk).

■ The poems in this collection are scary, the recipe isn't. These are heavy, greasy stick-to-your ribs olykoeks. Be sure to supervise the hot grease carefully, and use a long-handled spatula to lay the dough carefully in the electric frying pan. Consider using this donut recipe with *Homer Price* in the episode when the Doughnut Machine goes berserk, Viking: 0670377295 (hc), 0140309276 (pbk), or the out-of-print *Too Many Donuts* by Mark Alan Stamatky, Dial.

Ingredients
2 cans refrigerated biscuits
cooking oil
powdered sugar

Other
a film can to cut centers out

Directions
Pour 2 inches of cooking oil into an electric skillet or fry pan and heat. Ease the biscuits or olykoeks into the hot oil, and turn with a skewer. Drain on newspaper and dust with powdered sugar.

HELGA'S SAWDUST-FILLED WEDDING PASTRIES to

go with *Helga's Dowry: A Troll Love Story* by Tomie dePaola, Harcourt Brace: ISBN 0156400103 (pbk), 0152337016 (lb).

■ Helga is forced to earn her dowry to marry handsome Lars. One of her tasks is to cut down a forest, which certainly creates lots of sawdust. Once she's ready to marry Lars, she realizes there are better prospects around, and besides, now she's a wealthy woman!

Ingredients
2 pounds ground round
1 package Pepperidge Farm stuffing prepared according to package.

Directions
Divide meat into 24 portions. Have each student make two round thin patties of meat. Put a tablespoon of stuffing in the center of one meat patty and cover with another one. Pinch edges shut. Bake one hour at 350°F until meat is brown.

RUSSIAN TEA to go with
Here Comes the Cat by
Vladimir Vagin,
Scholastic: ISBN
0590418548 (hc)

■ The Cat and the Mouse share a cup of Russian tea in this story of international understanding that was written long before the demise of the Soviet Union.

Ingredients
2 cups sugar
2 cups Tang® (dry)
1 cup instant tea
1 package lemonade mix
1 teaspoon ground cloves
1 teaspoon ground cinnamon

Directions
Combine all well in a bowl, then keep in an airtight container. To make tea, use three tablespoons to a cup of hot water, stir to dissolve.

COW JUMPED OVER THE MOON CROISSANTS to
go with *Hey, Diddle Diddle* by Kin Eagle and Roby Gilbert, Charlesbridge: ISBN 1879085976 (hc).

■ These moon-shaped snacks (great for jumping over) are delicately flavored with "cow cheese."

Ingredients
2 packages refrigerated croissants
1 cup shredded cheese

Directions
Remove croissants from can, spread out on cookie sheet or clean surface. Separate along perforations, then cut each croissant in half so it makes two smaller triangles. Before you roll up the croissant (fat end first), sprinkle on about one tablespoon of shredded cheese. Place croissants on cookie sheet. Curve slightly to make into "moon" shapes. Bake at 350°F for about seven minutes, until browned on top.

EDIBLE ELEPHANT EGG NESTS to go with *Horton Hatches the Egg* by Dr. Seuss, Random House: ISBN 039480077X (hc).

■ Horton never loses hope of hatching his egg, because "an elephant never gives up." These steadfast little nests will hold jellybean eggs.

Ingredients
1 jar peanut butter
2 12-ounce bags chocolate chips
2 large cans or bags chowmein noodles
jelly beans

Other
wax paper

Directions
Melt peanut butter and chocolate chips in large bowl in microwave. Stir in chowmein noodles. Drop a handful-sized glob onto wax paper and form a nest with a little indentation in the middle for the "eggs." Let harden in refrigerator. Add jellybean "eggs" after the nests are firm.

CRABBY SALAD to go with *A House for Hermit Crab,* written and illustrated by Eric Carle, Simon & Schuster: ISBN 0887080561 (hc), 0887081681 (mini-edition), or *Why the Crab Has No Head: An African Folktale* by Barbara Knutson, Lerner/Carolrhoda: ISBN 0876143222 (lb).

■ This is a little labor-intensive to make, but looks like a crab when it's done.

Ingredients:
12 canned pear halves
24 canned peach slices
24 Maraschino cherries
1 box Nilla® wafers, crushed.

Other
12 paper plates
toothpicks

Directions
Put each pear half cut side down on a paper plate as the body of the crab. Put two peach slices for claws at the narrow end of the pear pointing toward the center. Put a cherry on the end of a toothpick and insert it into the narrow end of the pear, like an antenna. Do another antenna. Surround with a bed of "sand" made of crushed vanilla wafers.

UN-FRIED WORMS to go with *How to Eat Fried Worms* by Thomas Rockwell, illustrated by Emily A. McCully, Yearling: ISBN 0440445450 (pbk).

■ The bet is on! For $100, a kid can eat a worm a day, but the one putting up the money gets to choose the worm. You can make these "worms" really long and disgusting.

Ingredients

1 box red Jell-O®	1 jar baby food, plums
1 box green Jell-O	1 jar baby food, peaches
lettuce	

Directions

Combine red and green Jell-O (to make brown) and prepare using only the amount of liquid required for one box (half the regular amount). Let it set in the refrigerator in a long glass pan or on a cookie sheet. Cut the brown Jell-O into long thin strips to look like worms, and twist them as you lay them on a bed of lettuce so they really DO look like worms. Instead of ketchup (which the hero in the story uses to mask the taste of the worms) use baby food plums and instead of mustard use baby food peaches.

CHOCOLATE MOOSE MUFFINS to go with *If You Give a Moose a Muffin* by Laura Joffe Numeroff, illustrated by Felicia Bond, HarperCollins: ISBN 0060244054 (hc).

■ In this delightful circular story, every little moose ought to have a muffin. You could even make moose antlers for the kids out of brown paper bags if you like, and staple them to base-ball hats to make them wearable.

Ingredients

12 ready-made chocolate muffins
24 butterscotch chips for eyes
24 garden vegetable flavor crackers
12 fruit roll-ups

Directions

To make the moose's ears, cut fruit roll-ups into long, skinny triangles that measure about 1 inch long and 1/2 inch wide. Make a V-shaped slit in the top of the muffin for the ears, and insert the fruit roll-up pieces so they hang out over the edge of the muffin like moose ears. Using garden vegetable crackers that have wavy edges like moose antlers, stick two antlers into each cupcake beside of the ears. Add butterscotch chip eyes to the top of the cupcake.

NO-BAKE CHOCOLATE COOKIES to go with *If You Give a Mouse a Cookie* by Laura Joffe Numeroff, illustrated by Felicia Bond, HarperCollins: ISBN 0060245867 (hc), 0064434095 (big book).

■ Chances are, these cookies will make all your little readers thirsty for a glass of milk.

Ingredients

4 tablespoons instant cocoa
2 cups sugar
1/2 cup butter
1/2 cup milk

1/2 cup Rice Krispies®
2 teaspoons vanilla
1/2 cup peanut butter
3 cups one-minute oatmeal

Directions

Mix cocoa, sugar, butter, and milk in pot, and bring to a boil on low heat. Remove from heat and add peanut butter, vanilla, oats, and Rice Krispies. Mix together with a spoon. Drop small globs onto wax paper. They're ready to eat! And remember . . . if you give a mouse a cookie, chance are, he'll want some milk to go with it too!

EDIBLE GARDEN WITH WORMS to go with *Inch by Inch* by Leo Lionni, Mulberry Books: ISBN 0688132839 (pbk).

■ Have you noticed that there just aren't many good worm books out there? This could be a fun-filled activity to accompany any earthworm stories that do crawl into the library, or you could use it with just about any gardening book.

Ingredients

6 cups cold milk
2 6-ounce packages instant chocolate pudding
12 graham crackers
12 gummy worms

Other

12 clear plastic cups
12 Ziploc® baggies
12 plastic spoons

Directions

Put milk and pudding into bowl. Stir for two minutes. Pour equal portions of pudding into plastic cups. Put one graham cracker into each baggie, snap shut, and crush however you like. This is the "dirt," which you now put on top of the pudding. Insert gummy worm into the chocolate pudding "dirt" so its head is sticking out. Refrigerate until it's time for snack.

MICKEY'S MORNING CAKE to go with *In the Night Kitchen* by Maurice Sendak, HarperCollins: ISBN 0060266686 (hc), 0064434362 (pbk).

■ "We bake cake and nothing's the matter," the Night Kitchen Bakers chant while Mickey falls into the batter in the book; this is much quicker and less messy, but full of milk nonetheless.

Ingredients
2 cups Bisquick®   2 tablespoons sugar
2/3 cup milk   1 egg

Streusel Topping (mix together until crumb-like)
1/3 cup Bisquick
1/3 cup brown sugar
1/2 teaspoon cinnamon
2 tablespoons homemade butter (See **Homemade Butter** recipe
   entry to go with *Sam and the Tigers.*)

Directions
Mix ingredients (except Streusel Topping) about one minute by hand or with mixer. Spread in a greased baking dish. Mix ingredients for Streusel Topping together until crumblike, and then sprinkle over cake batter. Bake 20 minutes at 350°F or until toothpick comes out clean in center.

JACK'S RED-HANDED THREE-BEAN HOT DISH to go with *Jack and the Beanstalk* by Steven Kellogg, William Morrow: ISBN 0688102506 (hc), Mulberry Books: 0688152813 (pbk).

■ Jack slides down the beanstalk after his terrible deeds of derring-do in the giant's castle. Chances are, he knocks off a few beans along the way. This might be his mother's idea of a meal, but it's an easy snack.

Ingredients
1 can cut green beans
1 can garbanzo beans
1 can yellow wax beans
2 precooked boneless chicken breasts or 1 can of chicken
1 bag salt-and-vinegar potato chips

Directions
Drain the cans of beans and throw the liquid away. Stir the beans and chicken in a glass dish or casserole dish. Crush a small bag of salt-and-vinegar chips. Sprinkle the crumbs on the top of the bean and chicken casserole. Bake at 350°F for 20 minutes while the magic harp sings to you.

JACK'S BREAD PUDDING

to go with *Jack Takes the Cake* by Marni McGee, illustrated by Dana Regan, Troll Communications: ISBN 0816744351 (pbk).

■ Jack is a carefree boy who lives with his papa and his puppy not far from Granny's house. Jack visits her almost every day, and she usually gives him something to take home to his Papa. Unfortunately, Jack is a rather simple fellow—not very bright—and he has a way of getting things quite comically wrong. Papa says that Jack "has pudding where his brains should be." One of the silly things that Jack does is to stop beside the creek and dip a loaf of bread in the water before bringing it home to his Papa. Not the way to carry bread! In this recipe, soaking bread in liquid is the *right* thing to do. The custard soaks into the bread and when it's cooked, this pudding tastes a lot like cake. What could be better for Jack!

Ingredients:
2 large eggs
1/3 cup of milk
2 tablespoons of light brown sugar
2 tablespoons of frozen orange juice concentrate undiluted
6 slices of cinnamon raisin bread
1 tablespoons of butter
vanilla ice cream (about 1 cup) or sweet berry jam

Directions
Break eggs into a small bowl and whisk with a fork. Add milk, brown sugar, and orange juice. Mix together and pour into an oblong, glass container. Place bread slices into the custard mixture; turn them over to make sure they are soaked. Melt the butter on a pancake griddle (or in two large skillets). Cook the custard-bread over medium heat until golden brown on the bottom. This will take about five minutes. Carefully turn the slices over (they tend to break apart because they're soggy) and cook the other side for four or five minutes more. Cut each slice into triangles or strips. Arrange on dessert plates and top with vanilla ice cream or a dollop of jam. Serve immediately. Contributed by the author.

JAMBERRY PARFAITS
to go with *Jamberry*
by Bruce Degen,
HarperFestival: ISBN
0694006513 (bd).

■ Enjoy the layers of rhyme in this easy reader, as well as the layers of flavor in this jam-filled treat!

Ingredients
3 big containers vanilla yogurt
1 package frozen strawberries thawed
12 Teddy Grahams crackers

Other
12 clear plastic cups
12 plastic spoons

Directions
Layer yogurt and strawberries in cups, top with a Teddy Graham and eat.

COLD NORTH ATLANTIC
PEACH SLUSH to go with
James and the Giant Peach by Roald Dahl,
Knopf: ISBN 0679880909
(hc), Penguin:
0140374248 (pbk)

■ While the sharks are gnawing away at the bottom of the fruity frigate somewhere east of Nova Scotia, this would be an appropriate snack for all aboard the peach to contemplate.

Ingredients
12 cans of snack-size peaches
1 quart milk
36 ice cubes
cinnamon

Other
12 plastic cups
blender

Directions
Let each kid open a can of peaches, pour into the blender and add another can of milk and three ice cubes. Blend for about 10 seconds and pour into a cup, sprinkle on a shake of cinnamon. Serve with spoons.

JAMES HENRY TROTTER'S MESS from

James and the Giant Peach by Roald Dahl, Knopf: ISBN 0679880909 (hc), Penguin: 0140374248 (pbk).

■ Poor James never gets to make this recipe that would free him from the tyranny of Aunt Sponge and Aunt Spiker because he drops a bag under a peach tree. The following recipe appears in Chapter Three of the story: "100 Long, Slimy Crocodile tongues boiled up in the skull of a dead witch for 21 days and nights with the eyeballs of a lizard. Add the fingers of a dead monkey, the gizzard of a pig, the beak of a green parrot, the juice of a porcupine, and three spoonfuls of sugar. Stew for another week and let the moon do the rest."

Ingredients
100 crocodile tongues
2 lizard eyeballs
10 dead monkey fingers
1 pig gizzard
1 green parrot beak
1 porcupine, juiced
3 spoonfuls sugar
water to cover

Directions
Read this recipe to the kids and ask them to brainstorm what real world ingredients could possibly be substituted for each item in the horrible recipe. Once you get a workable recipe, ask them to figure out a way to adapt the time scale so that it doesn't all turn into a science project that will kill anybody who comes near it. And how are we going to boil it up without a witch's skull? Perhaps a big white baking or casserole dish will have to do. Once they've accomplished this stupendous task of lateral thinking, they're on the way to writing their OWN cookbook of literary recipes. Please send me a copy!

JAMIE O'ROURKE'S SMASHED POTATOES

to go with *Jamie O'Rourke and the Big Potato* by Tomie dePaola, Putnam: ISBN 039922257X (hc).

■ The laziest man alive, Jamie likes this Irish snack—except he thinks mashing those potatoes takes too much work.

Ingredients

12 large slices of boiled ham
12 large potatoes, cooked to mashing consistency
milk
butter
parsley sprigs

Directions

Potatoes could be cooked to mashing consistency as part of the activity, or you could precook them (or even use instant potatoes if you're really incredibly lazy). Whatever way you choose, let each child mash the potato in a bowl with about two tablespoons of milk and a small pat of butter using a fork. In a twelve-hole muffin tin, line the sides and bottom with the boiled ham slice. (Use metal cupcake papers if you can find them to reduce the cleanup time.) Fill each ham hollow about 2/3 full with mashed potatoes. Bake at 300°F for about 20 minutes. Add a sprig of fresh parsley (for a touch of green) just before serving.

JAMIE O'ROURKE'S LAZY LASAGNA to go
with *Jamie O'Rourke and the Pooka* by Tomie dePaola, Putnam: ISBN 0399234675 (hc).

■ Even though Jamie's wife leaves him lots of food, his free-loading buddies polish it all off. He makes a big mess in the kitchen for his wife to clean up after the Pooka (Irish animal spirit) deserts him. This can easily make a big mess too.

Ingredients
2 jars spaghetti sauce
1 box lasagna noodles
1 large container cottage cheese or ricotta

1 large container yogurt
1 package sliced mozzarella cheese
1/2 cup grated Parmesan cheese
1/2 cup water

Directions
In a 13x9 baking pan, layer one cup spaghetti sauce, one layer dry lasagna noodles, one layer of cottage cheese, one layer of yogurt, one layer of mozzarella, one layer of spaghetti sauce, one layer of lasagna noodles, one layer of cottage cheese, one layer of yogurt, and finally one layer of mozzarella. You probably feel as frazzled as Jamie does! Finish with a layer of spaghetti sauce. Pour water around the edges. Cover tightly with foil. Bake at 350°F about an hour, or until your friends come over to party. Let it stand 20 minutes before serving, just long enough for the Pooka to come clean up the mess.

MR. CHAPMAN'S FAMOUS APPLESAUCE
to go with *Johnny Appleseed* by Steven Kellogg, William Morrow: ISBN 0688064183 (hc).

■ Applesauce can be made from any kind of apples. Traditionally, windfalls were used because they wouldn't keep very long otherwise. Perhaps you have a local orchard where kids can pick up windfalls, or maybe you can ask the local grocer to save you some bruised apples.

Ingredients
12 apples (peeled and cored, sliced and diced with hurt parts cut out)
1 cup sugar
1/2 cup raisins

1 teaspoon ground cinnamon
1 cup water
1/2 stick butter

Directions
Mix everything well and put into baking dish, cover with foil (or use a lid if you're lucky enough to have one that fits tightly). Bake for about two-and-a-half hours. Take off foil and bake another 30 minutes. Serve warm with Cool Whip or whipped cream.

FISH BALLS to go with *Just Me and My Dad* by Mercer Mayer, Golden Books: ISBN 0307118398 (pbk).

■ Camping and fishing are "guy" things in the story—but the guys don't catch any fish! So these are "fishless" fish balls.

Ingredients
4 tablespoons vegetable oil
1 tablespoon butter
1 onion, finely chopped
1 pound ground beef
2 handfuls grated carrot
1 tablespoon chopped fresh parsley
1 tablespoon sugar
1 egg beaten
1 tablespoon flour

Directions
In an electric skillet, melt together vegetable oil and butter, then sauté chopped onion. In a bowl, moosh together ground beef, carrot, parsley, sugar, egg, and flour. Make into balls, and then cook until browned in the same skillet in which you sautéed the onions.

MOUSEOPOLIS TUNA SNACK to go with *Kat Kong* by Dav Pilkey, Harcourt Brace: ISBN 0152420363 (hc), 0152420371 (pbk).

■ The fearless mice lure the monster with this snack and vanquish him forever.

Ingredients
3 cans tuna, drained
1 container Hidden Valley Ranch salad dressing
1 can chopped black olives, drained
24 slices bread

Directions
Mix the tuna with enough salad dressing to make it spreadable. Add chopped olives to represent Kat Kong who has been conquered by the mice of Mouseopolis. Mix together gently and spread on 12 slices of bread, top with other slices of bread.

KANGAROO SANDWICHES to go with *Katy No Pocket* by Emmy Payne, illustrated by H.A. Rey, Houghton Mifflin: ISBN 0395171040 (lb), Sandpiper:

■ Katy may not have a pocket or pouch, but she can use these pitas to hold her lunch.

Ingredients
6 pitas, cut in half

Outback Filling:
The outback of Australia (where kangaroos live) is noted for its sheep camps, its red center, and songs the Aborigines alone can sing. In that spirit, we make this filling to stuff the pitas:

6 jars lamb baby food
2 cans red kidney beans (the red center), drained
1 package feta cheese crumbles (feta is made from sheep milk)

Directions
Smear the inside of the pita pocket with lamb baby food using a spoon (too messy for fingers). Add about two tablespoons of drained kidney beans. Add sprinkles of feta cheese (it's pretty strong stuff and kids tend to balk at the flavor if you use too much). Pinch the pita shut at the cut edge with fingers, nuke for about 30 seconds to warm, and then eat.

KING ARTHUR'S SHISH KEBABS on a sword to go with *King Arthur: The Sword in the Stone* by Hudson Talbott, William Morrow: ISBN 0688094031 (hc).

■ These little swords-in-the-stones are fun to eat and fun to make.

Ingredients
6 bratwurst, precooked, or 6 precooked hot dogs, sliced into "coins"
6 dried apricots or cherries, cut into small pieces
24 cheese cubes (dice-sized)
potatoes, cut in half to be the "stone"

Other
12 cocktail swords (or if they're hard to find, use tooth-flossing picks)

Directions
On a little plastic cocktail sword, layer ingredients until the sword is full, stick it into a potato half "rock," from which the budding King Arthurs can pull it.

LANCELOT'S MEAL ON A LANCE to go with
Lancelot: Tales of King Arthur by Hudson Talbott, William Morrow: ISBN 0688148328.

■ Create these fruity treats King Arthur's most notorious knight would love.

Ingredients
pineapple chunks
marshmallows
maraschino cherries

Other
12 cocktail swords or tooth-flossing picks

Directions
Layer ingredients on a cocktail sword, until the sword is full.

RAVEN HANNAH'S MAPLE APPLES to go with
Least of All by Carol Purdy, illustrated by Tim Arnold, Macmillan: ISBN 0689505057 (hc), Aladdin: 0689716818 (pbk).

■ These treats are Raven Hannah's favorites in the story.

Ingredients
1 quart sliced cored apples, not peeled
1 teaspoon ground cinnamon
1/2 cup raisins
3 tablespoons maple syrup
milk or vanilla ice cream (optional)

Directions
Nearly fill a four-quart crock-pot with cored sliced apples, leaving on the peel. Any variety of apple is good in the recipe. Add ground cinnamon, raisins, and maple syrup. Stir carefully until all ingredients are well mixed. Cook on high for two hours and continue cooking two additional hours on low. Stir well and serve warm with milk or vanilla ice cream. Store any leftovers in the refrigerator and enjoy them cold the next day. Contributed by Carol Purdy.

SANTA FE TRAIL CORNBREAD from *Lewis and Paper: Adventure on the Santa Fe Trail* by Barbara Joosse, illustrated by Jon Van Zyle, Chronicle: ISBN 0811819590 (hc)

■ Lewis and Papa leave Wisconsin and take the Santa Fe Trail to make their fortune. Along the way, they eat trail food, which would have, of course, included cornbread such as this.

Ingredients
1 cup sifted flour
1/4 cup sugar
4 teaspoons baking powder
3/4 teaspoon salt
1 cup yellow cornmeal
2 eggs
1 cup milk
1/4 cup shortening

Directions
Sift flour with sugar, baking powder, cornmeal, and salt. Add eggs, milk, and shortening. Beat until smooth (but don't beat too much). Pour into greased 9x9x2-inch pan. Bake at 425°F for 20-25 minutes. Cut into 12 pieces. Contributed by Barbara Joosse.

SANTA FE TRAIL SPOON BREAD from *Lewis and Paper: Adventure on the Santa Fe Trail* by Barbara Joosse, illustrated by Jon Van Zyle, Chronicle: ISBN 0811819590.

■ During their journey along the Santa Fe Trail, Lewis and Papa would have enjoyed spoon bread.

Ingredients
1 cup cornmeal
2 cups milk
1 teaspoon salt
1 teaspoon baking powder
2 tablespoons oil
1 cup milk
3 eggs separated
butter

Directions
Cook cornmeal in two cups of milk till it's the consistency of mush. Remove from heat. Add salt, baking powder, oil, and one cup milk. Add three well-beaten egg yolks. Fold in three stiffly beaten egg whites. Bake in greased two-quart casserole at 325°F for one hour. Spoon into warm dishes, top with butter. Contributed by Barbara Joosse.

APPLE BUTTER YOU MAKE IN THE OVEN to go

with *Life and Times of the Apple* by Charles Micucci, Orchard: ISBN 0521059391 (hc).

■ After you learn about the life cycle of an apple tree, hardly a moment passes before this long-cooking apple butter is done.

Ingredients
5 quarts applesauce, unsweetened
10 cups sugar
1 cup vinegar
2 teaspoons ground cinnamon
1 teaspoon ground cloves

Directions
Combine ingredients in large, greased roasting pan. Bake at 350°F for three hours until thick. Stir every 20 minutes. Pour into jars and seal. Makes about six quarts total, enough for each student to have a pint to take home and share.

BUNNY RABBIT HEAVEN CARROT SALAD to go

with *Lip Lap's Wish* by Jonathan London, illustrated by Sylvia Long, Chronicle: ISBN 0811805050 (hc), 0811818101 (pbk).

■ All good bunnies go to heaven and probably feast endlessly on salad like this.

Ingredients
12 carrots, shredded
1 cup Miracle Whip®
parsley sprigs
raisins
lettuce leaves

Directions
Mix shredded carrots with Miracle Whip, serve in a little carrot-shaped mound on a "lettuce leaf plate." Stick a piece of parsley in the top of the "carrot."

LIP LAP'S WISHING STARS to go with *Lip Lap's Wish* by Jonathan London, illustrated by Sylvia Long, Chronicle: ISBN 0811805050 (hc), 0811818101 (pbk).

■ Even sad, little bunnies wishing very hard will eat a salad of carrots and oranges. These will remind your *Lip Lap* readers of the stars in the sky.

Ingredients
2 containers soft Philadelphia cream cheese
1 small carrot, grated
1 can mandarin oranges drained
1 teaspoon powdered ginger
1 loaf white bread, thin-sliced

Other
star-shaped cookie cutter

Directions
Mix all these lovely ingredients together well, and spread on a nutritious slice of white bread. Cover with another piece of white bread and cut out with a star-shaped cookie cutter.

COMPLEMENTARY COLOR SNACKS to go with *Little Blue and Little Yellow: A Story for Pippo and Other Children* by Leo Lionni, Mulberry Books: ISBN 0688132855 (pbk).

■ Learn about color combinations with layers of blue and yellow.

Ingredients
1 package blue Jell-O®
1 package yellow Jell-O

Directions
Mix each batch of Jell-O separately, using only *half* as much liquid as required in directions. Pour about one tablespoon of the blue mixture into each muffin paper in a muffin pan. Let it set (about 45 minutes). Pour in yellow mixture, and be careful not to let colors blend too much. Let yellow set. Continue until all Jell-O is layered. Cool in refrigerator for about an hour and then serve.

LITTLE BOY BLUE POPCORN to go with

Little Boy Blue and Other Rhymes by Iona Opie, illustrated by Rosemary Wells, Candlewick Press: ISBN 0763603546 (board book).

■ Little Boy Blue would probably wake up *and* blow his horn for this snack.

Ingredients
blue corn popcorn
blue cake-decorating sugar sprinkles
1 box Bugles® crackers

Directions
Make blue popcorn in your favorite corn popper. Add blue cake-decorating sprinkles after the popcorn cools down a bit. Add Bugles crackers, which look very much like Little Boy Blue's horn. Mix together and munch.

JUNGLE ORANGE JULIUS

to go with *Little Gorilla* by Ruth Bornstein, Houghton Mifflin: ISBN 0899194214 (pbk), 0395287731 (lb).

■ Little Gorilla grows bigger and bigger, but everybody still loves him and comes to sing, "Happy Birthday, Little Gorilla." Your Little Gorillas will love this jungle treat.

Ingredients
1 can frozen undiluted orange juice
2 eggs
1 cup milk
4 tablespoons sugar
1 teaspoon vanilla extract
24 ice cubes

Directions
Blend until frothy, serve in a paper cup with a little party umbrella on it for Little Gorilla's birthday party.

APHRODITE'S MEXICAN SHRIMP ROLL-UPS to go

with *The Little Mermaid* by Hans Christian Andersen, illustrated by Charles Santore, Random House: ISBN 0157064952 (hc).

■ These tasty undersea treats resemble a mermaid's favorite dinner.

Ingredients

12 flour tortillas
3 cans bean dip

1 cup shredded cheese
1 can tiny shrimp, drained

Directions

On a tortilla, spread about two tablespoons bean dip and sprinkle with a handful of shredded cheese. Add about two tablespoons drained shrimp. Nuke for 30 seconds. Fold in half, nuke for 30 seconds. Let it cool before serving. Contributed by Chris Cole.

HOMEMADE CHEESE to

go with *Little Miss Muffet: And Other Nursery Rhymes,* illustrated by Lucy Cousins, Dutton: ISBN 0525457496 (hc).

■ Most kids aren't familiar with "curds and whey," and I'm not sure anybody has a clue what a tuffet is. This homemade cheese is actually like farmer's cheese.

Ingredients

1 gallon milk
1 Junket rennet tablet

Other

thermometer
cheese press (or you can make do with two clean boards and
     a couple of bricks)

Directions

One gallon milk yields one pound cheese. Allow milk to set to room temperature. Dissolve one Junket tablet in a tablespoon of milk, and then add to the gallon of milk in a large pot. After about an hour, a thin layer of whey appears on top and the curds settle on the bottom. Cut the curds—the smaller they are, the drier the cheese. Mix with a wooden spoon for about 10 minutes (you could have each child do one minute). Slowly heat while stirring, taking care not to heat it too fast. There should be a two-degree rise every five minutes maximum, and a temperature of no more than 102°F maximum. Put curds in cheese cloth and place in cheese press. Add more weight each day and turn twice a day. In about two weeks, you have farmer's cheese.

YUMMY CURDS AND WHEY to go with *Little Miss Muffet: And Other Nursery Rhymes*, illustrated by Lucy Cousins, Dutton: ISBN 0525457496 (hc).

■ Everybody knows that Miss Muffet didn't get to finish her snack. Maybe it wasn't as tasty as this version of curds and whey.

Ingredients
1 quart whole milk
1 Junket rennet tablet
3 tablespoons water

Directions
Warm the milk slowly in a pan or nuke it to 98°F. It cannot be hotter than body temperature or the rennet will not work. Crush up rennet tablet with water. Add to body-temperature milk. Let it set for about 20 minutes. Slice and drain in a colander lined with a coffee filters or cheesecloth. After the whey has drained out, you can add salt, sugar, or syrup, or just eat it plain. You should probably sit on tuffets while you eat this.

STRAWBERRY FEAST to go with *The Little Mouse, the Red Ripe Strawberry, and the Big, Hungry Bear* by Audrey Wood, Child's Play: ISBN 0859531821 (hc), 0859530124 (pbk).

■ The little mouse discovers that the *only* way to hide the strawberry from the big, hungry bear is the BEST way—to eat it! Students will enjoy eating these strawberries before the big, hungry bear gets them.

Ingredients
12 fresh, big, huge strawberries
1 container sour cream or unflavored yogurt
1 cup powdered sugar
1 cup brown sugar
1 can whipped cream
1 container Smucker's Magic Shell fudge ice cream topping

Directions
Wash strawberries. Set up separate little bowls or saucers with sour cream, yogurt, sugar, whipped cream, and fudge topping. If you have 12 kids, divide them into groups of four or six, sit them in a circle around the dipping bowls. In an orderly fashion, have students dip washed strawberries into the various toppings by holding on to the hulls.

WHOLE WHEAT BREAD

to go with *The Little Red Hen* by Paul Galdone, Houghton Mifflin: ISBN 0395288037 (hc), 08991934948 (pbk).

■ This requires a bread machine. "Somebody is sure to have one you can borrow," said the Little Red Hen.

Ingredients.
1 small container plain yogurt
1/4 cup warm water
1 tablespoon vegetable oil
2 tablespoons maple syrup (pancake syrup will do)
1 cup whole wheat flour
2 cups bread flour (it's different from regular flour)
2 tablespoons wheat germ
1 teaspoon salt
1 package quick-rise yeast

Directions
Add everything in the order listed into a bread maker "bucket." Set bread maker machine to "dough" setting (it doesn't bake it, only mixes and kneads it and takes it through the first rise). After the first rise, take the dough out of the little bucket and put it on a floured board. Knead it for a while. Let every kid have a chance to knead it for a minute or so, or while they count as high as they can. Roll out to a long snake. Cut dough with scissors into 12 sections, one per student. Make into little "loaf" shapes. Put on a cookie sheet, cover with a clean towel, and let rise in a warm, draft-free place about one hour. Bake at 350°F until the loaves are brown and sound "hollow" when you tap them. This would be yummy with homemade butter (*See the* **Homemade Butter** *entry that goes with* **Sam and the Tigers**).

SHORTCUT CAKE to go with *Little Red Riding Hood*, illustrated by Trina Schart Hyman, Holiday House: ISBN 0823406539 (pbk), 0823404706 (lb).

■ Little Red took the shortcut to Granny's, and we all know what happened. We hope this recipe turns out better.

Ingredients
1 1/2 cups flour
1 cup sugar
1/4 cup cocoa
2 teaspoons instant coffee
1 teaspoon baking soda
1/2 teaspoon salt
6 tablespoons oil
1 tablespoon vinegar
1 teaspoon vanilla
1 cup cold water

Directions
Put all dry ingredients into an 8-inch square baking pan. Stir together with a fork to mix them up well. With your fingers, make a little well in three different places in the dry stuff. In the first hole, pour the oil, in the second hole pour the vinegar and in the third hole pour the vanilla. Now pour the water carefully over the whole thing. Use fork to mix everything together well. You cannot over-mix this. Bake at 350°F for 40 minutes, until it just starts to pull away from the sides of the pan. Cool in the pan. When cool, cut into 12 pieces and serve.

SHREDDED WOLF DIP AND CHIPS to go with *Little Red Riding Hood* by William Wegman, Hyperion: ISBN 1562824163 (hc),1562824171 (lb).

■ If Little Red Riding Hood had known about this dip, she and Grandma would have *had* a dinner party and not *been* one.

Ingredients
1 small jar dried beef slices (cut up into teeny-tiny strips with clean scissors; this is the shredded wolf part)
1 package Hidden Valley Ranch dressing mix
2 cups mayonnaise
2 cups sour cream
red tortilla chips (which are seasonally available, otherwise use Doritos®)

Directions
Mix everything together in a bowl and let the flavors blend in the refrigerator for a couple of hours. Serve with red tortilla chips, which Little Red Riding Hood would like.

TWELVE LITTLE GIRLS IN TWO STRAIGHT LINES

to go with *Mad About Madeline: The Complete Tales* by Ludwig Bemelmans, Viking: ISBN 0670851876 (hc).

■ Miss Clavelle would like this tidy, symmetrical snack that looks like 12 little girls in two straight lines.

Ingredients
12 cannelloni
1 large container cottage cheese or ricotta
1 tablespoon onion salt
1 teaspoon dried parsley
1 1/2 cups shredded white cheese (such as Monterey Jack)
12 cheese slices
1/2 cup spaghetti sauce
24 olives
12 pimentos

Directions
Mix cottage cheese, onion salt, parsley, and one cup of shredded Monterey Jack cheese well. Stuff mixture inside uncooked cannelloni. Place 12 stuffed cannelloni in a glass baking dish (line them up like Madeline and the little girls all asleep). Add a blanket of cheese slices, then add a stripe of spaghetti sauce along the top. Above this, add olives for the heads with shredded cheese hair and pimento lips. For feet, position olive halves at the end of the blanket.

MS. FRIZZLE'S UNDERSEA DINNER

to go with *The Magic School Bus on the Ocean Floor* by Joanna Cole, illustrated by Bruce Degen, Scholastic: ISBN 0590414305 (hc), 0590414313 (pbk).

■ This undersea treat could be used with other fish- and ocean-related stories as well.

Ingredients
1 package pasta seashells
1 large can tuna packed in water
1 can cream of mushroom soup
1 can milk
1 sheet Nori roasted seaweed (cut into long, skinny strips)
Pepperidge Farm® Goldfish® crackers

Directions
Mix everything together in a large, ovenproof casserole dish (no need to cook the pasta). Make sure it is well distributed, as you're creating an ecosystem here. Bake one hour at 325°F, or until pasta is al dente. Put a "school" of Goldfish crackers on top of casserole.

QUALITY TIME POPCORN/MOMCORN

to go with *Make Way for Dumb Bunnies* by Sue Denim, illustrated by Dav Pilkey, Scholastic: ISBN 0590582860 (hc).

■ The Dumb Bunnies' favorite snack is popcorn (and "momcorn").

Ingredients
4 bags microwavable popcorn
parmesan cheese
pepper sprinkles

Other
12 Ziploc® bags

Directions
After microwaving popcorn, combine some popcorn, a few shakes of cheese, and a few pepper sprinkles in a Ziploc bag. Seal the bag shut and shake well before eating.

PICKLE JUICE PANCAKES

to go with *Vinegar Pancakes and Vanishing Cream* by Bonnie Pryor, illustrated by Gail Owens, HarperCollins/William Morrow: ISBN 068806728X (hc), 0688147445 (pbk).

■ In the story, the kids try to make breakfast for their parents using pickle juice and flour to make pancakes. This is a tastier recipe, and it's much more edible.

Ingredients
3 cups flour
3 teaspoons sugar
1 1/2 teaspoons salt
3/4 teaspoon baking powder
1/2 teaspoon baking soda
3 eggs
3 cups buttermilk (if you don't have buttermilk, add three teaspoons of vinegar (pickle juice will do nicely too) to three cups milk and stir; this turns into "buttermilk" after standing for about five minutes)
6 tablespoons melted butter
maple syrup or fruit syrup

Directions
Sift together flour with sugar, salt, baking powder, and baking soda. In another bowl, beat three eggs and add buttermilk. Add melted butter. Stir wet mixture into dry mixture. A few small lumps should remain. Fry on a very hot griddle and serve with butter and maple or fruit syrup. Contributed by Bonnie Pryor.

UNLAMB SHISH KEBABS

to go with *Mary Had a Little Lamb* by Sarah Josepha Hale, illustrated by Tomie dePaola, Holiday House: ISBN 0823405095 (lb)

■ Youngsters generally won't eat shish kebabs made with real lamb, so these will suffice nicely.

Ingredients
1 package tofu cut into cubes
1 small can cooked canned whole potatoes
1 small can cooked canned whole carrots
1 small can cooked canned whole onions
36 pieces of green pepper
mint jelly thinned to consistency of maple syrup

Other
12 wooden skewers

Directions
Place each ingredient on a skewer. Nuke at 50% for two minutes. Brush mint jelly onto "lamb."

CHICKENLESS HOMEMADE FUDGE to go

with *Max's Chocolate Chicken* by Rosemary Wells, Dial: ISBN 0670887137 (hc).

■ Max and Ruby have an Easter candy hunt and search for the elusive Chocolate Chicken. Shape these fudge treats into chicken shapes with a cookie cutter if you have one.

Ingredients
1 stick butter
1 box powdered sugar
1/2 cup cocoa
1/4 cup milk
1 teaspoon vanilla

Directions
Nuke the butter until melted. Add sugar, cocoa, milk, vanilla. Stir until well blended. Press into 8-inch square dish. Refrigerate until firm. Cut into Max-sized pieces. If you prefer to have each youngster have a separate serving, you can put about two spoonfuls into a cupcake paper in a muffin tin instead of using the large container.

OLD HAIRY "EAT-ONE-AND-DIE" COOKIES from

Mayfield Crossing by Vaunda Micheaux Nelson, illustrated by Leonard Jenkins, Putnam: ISBN 0399223312 (hc), Camelot 0380721791 (pbk), Econo-Clad: 0785720723 (lb).

■ When Mama puts walnuts that she bought from Scary Old Hairy in her chocolate chip cookies, Meg, Billie, and their friends think they might be poisoned (see Chapters Five and Six).

Ingredients
2 cups flour
1 teaspoon soda
1 teaspoon salt
1 cup soft butter (NOT margarine)
3/4 cup white sugar
3/4 cup brown sugar (packed)
1 teaspoon vanilla
2 eggs
1 6-ounce package chocolate chips
walnuts

Directions
Combine flour, soda, and salt. Set aside. Cream together butter, white and brown sugar, vanilla, and eggs. Stir in dry ingredients. Add nuts, roughly chopped. Drop by teaspoonfuls onto a nonstick or greased cookie sheet and bake at 375°F for five to seven minutes. Cookies should flatten out and be thin and chewy. They may seem a bit underdone, but will firm up as they cool. If they are baked too long they will get crunchy when cool. Contributed by Vaunda Nelson.

OPEN-FACE ROOSTER SANDWICHES to go with

El Medio Pollito/The Half Chick by Rosario Ferre, Santillana Publishing: ISBN 9681902998 (pbk), or *Mediopollito/Half-Chicken* by Alma Flor Ada, Doubleday Dell: 0606116125 (hc).

■ Each version of the traditional Spanish folk tale about the weathervane chicken "Medio Pollito," or Half-Chicken, reveal why he sits atop barns and houses instead of running around like other chickens.

Ingredients

6 hard-boiled eggs
6 tablespoons mayonnaise or
    Miracle Whip®
24 pickle slices cut into triangles
24 slices bread
12 raisins
12 carrot pieces to look like a rooster's beak
chicken- or rooster-shaped cookie cutter
skinny pretzel sticks

Directions

First, make the egg salad. Peel the hard-boiled eggs and chop up into fine pieces in a bowl using two knives (or an egg slicer if you have one). Add enough mayonnaise or Miracle Whip to make it the consistency of peanut butter. Cut bread using chicken/rooster cookie cutter. Spread completely with egg salad, then add little tiny pickle slice triangles for the wing, a raisin for the eyes and a piece of a carrot cut into a small triangle for the beak. Add a pretzel stick for the weathervane and you have a lovely edible two-dimensional Medio Pollito.

"SPIDER" CIDER to go with *Miss Spider's Tea Party* by David Kirk, Scholastic: ISBN 0590477242 (hc), also available with a tea set: ISBN 0590129945.

■ Miss Spider can't figure out why nobody wants to have tea with her. They all think that they're being invited to *be* lunch instead of to *have* lunch! A child called this drink "Spider," an interesting portmanteau word made up of "spiced" and "cider." The perfect drink for a spidery tea time. Of course you could use this with all the *Miss Spider* books as well as other arachnid tales.

Ingredients
1 small jar of Tang®
1 small jar of powdered instant iced tea
1 tablespoon ground cinnamon

Directions
Mix Tang, iced tea mix, and cinnamon together in a large bowl, then transfer to a canister or airtight container like an empty coffee can. To make each drink, put three heaping spoonfuls of mix in a coffee cup, add hot water, and stir.

TROPICAL PARADISE SMOOTHIES to go with *Moe the Dog in Tropical Paradise* by Diane Stanley, illustrated by Elise Primavera, PaperStar: ISBN 0698117611 (pbk).

■ Arlene and Moe hate the winter and dream of a vacation on the beach with palm trees, but they settle for the tropical atmosphere created while they sip these tangy drinks.

Ingredients (for each child)
one container yogurt, any flavor
one banana
4 ice cubes
1 serving orange juice or Sunny Delight®

Other
clear plastic drinking cups
straw
little cocktail umbrella to stick in the drinks

Directions
Each child gets to be Moe the Dog and make a wonderful smoothie for himself and Arlene. Put the container of yogurt in the blender, add peeled banana, add four ice cubes. Fill empty yogurt container with Sunny Delight or orange juice, add to blender. Blend until it's smooth and thick. Pour into plastic cup, add a straw and a cocktail umbrella.

PASTA PRIMO to go with *More Spaghetti I Say* by Rita Golden Gelman, illustrated by Kent Cook, Scholastic: ISBN 0590714392 (pbk).

■ This easy reader is a great incentive to eat more spaghetti. This recipe could easily go with Strega Nona and Big Anthony's many exploits in *Strega Nona* by Tomie dePaola, Aladdin: ISBN 0671666061 (pbk).

Ingredients
1 package spaghetti
1 stick butter (cut into pats)
1 container grated Parmesan cheese

Directions
Cook spaghetti according to directions. When it's done to about al dente consistency, drain. Cut stick of butter in to pats (students get good practice cutting with table knives), and add to spaghetti. Let the butter melt. Using a spaghetti "rake," serve each kid "more-spaghetti-I-say" in a paper bowl. Let them shake on their own Parmesan cheese. Did you tell your students that one way to test the doneness of spaghetti is to throw a strand at the ceiling? If it sticks, it's done—a little messy, but fun.

MULTICOLOR JUNKET to go with *Mouse Paint* by Ellen Stoll Walsh, Harcourt Brace: ISBN 0152001182 (pbk), 0152002650 (board book), 0152560262 (big book).

■ In the Mouse World, you can play with colors and then disappear into whiteness to outwit the cat. Here's an edible version that kids can play with too. Look for little gray jellybeans to put on top as "mice."

Ingredients
2 Junket rennet tablets
6 cups milk
2 cups powdered milk
6 tablespoons honey
food coloring
gray jellybeans (hard to find)

Directions
Combine milk, powdered milk, and honey in a saucepan. Heat to only 100°F. In a cup, dissolve rennet tablets in a tablespoon of water. Stir rennet mixture into milk; stir seven times. Pour into 12 custard cups or clear plastic cups (1/2 cup each). Add one drop of red, yellow, and blue food color to the top of each cup. Stir one time. Do not move the cups until the junket sets. The colors kind of settle into pools like the colors in the book.

GHOST IN A CAVE COOKIES to go with

Mrs. Jeepers' Secret Cave by Debbie Dadey and Marcia Thornton Jones, illustrated by John Steve Gurney, Scholastic: ISBN 0590189816 (pbk).

■ The spooky ghosts on the cookies are the only scary thing about these snacks.

Ingredients
2 sticks of butter, softened
1 1/2 cups sugar
2 eggs
2 teaspoons vanilla extract
2 cups all purpose flour
2/3 cup unsweetened cocoa
1 teaspoon baking soda
1/4 teaspoon salt
1/4 cup powdered sugar
red sprinkles

Directions
In a large bowl, beat butter, sugar, eggs, and vanilla together until fluffy. In a small bowl, mix flour, cocoa, baking soda, and salt, and then stir into butter mixture. Drop by rounded teaspoonfuls onto a cookie sheet. Flatten each ball of dough with a knife or spatula. Bake from eight to 10 minutes at 350°F. Let the cookies cool slightly, and then set on a plate. Draw a ghost on a piece of wax paper. Cut out the outline of the ghost on the wax paper to make a stencil. Place the wax paper stencil on top of a cookie and gently shake the powdered sugar over the cookie. Remove the stencil and give each ghost two red sprinkle eyes. Makes about four to five dozen spookily delicious cookies! Contributed by Marcia Thornton Jones and Debbie Dadey.

WEDDING DAY CORN MUSH to go with *A Navajo Wedding Day: A Diné Marriage Ceremony,* written and illustrated by Eleanor Schick, Marshall Cavendish: ISBN 0761450319 (hc).

■ Corn mush is used in the traditional Diné (Navajo) marriage ceremony. The women of the Bitterwater Clan in Shonto, Arizona, where the wedding in Navajo Wedding Day takes place use white cornmeal. They say, "Corn is life, and white is the color of the East where everything begins." In their ceremony, the corn mush is set in the center of the wedding basket. The person performing the ceremony—an uncle of the bride or a medicine man—sprinkles corn pollen across the corn mush in a line from east to west and from south to north to honor the four sacred mountains that surround their land. The officiator then sprinkles a circle of corn pollen around the edge of the corn mush, leaving an opening at the East. The bride and groom each eat some corn mush from the east side of the basket and then from the south side, then from the west side, and then from the north side. Then they eat some from the center. After this, the groom's relatives come up and eat some too. In the wedding ceremony, the corn mush is not sweetened. You can eat it plain or make a tasty breakfast cereal or snack by topping it with maple syrup, honey, or sugar.

Ingredients
3 cups coarse ground cornmeal
3 cups cold water
3 teaspoons salt

Directions
Combine cornmeal and salt. Bring water to a boil. Stir cornmeal mixture gradually into water so it never stops boiling. Cook the mush over quick heat for two to three minutes, stirring constantly so it doesn't stick and burn. Then place over boiling water in double boiler and steam about 15 minutes, stirring frequently. Contributed by Eleanor Schick.

GRILLED CHEESE WITH A DIFFERENCE from *The New Complete Babysitter's Handbook* by Carol Barkin and Elizabeth James, illustrated by Martha Weston, Clarion: ISBN 0395665574 (hc), 0395665582 (pbk).

■ This nifty handbook for young babysitters offers an easy recipe to feed hungry youngsters. All you need for this quick variation on grilled cheese sandwiches are tortillas and cheese. It takes very little time to put together, it's not too messy, and it's not "junk food"—but it's food that children love.

Ingredients
12 tortillas
sliced cheese (Monterey Jack is best, but Colby or
    American would do)

Directions
Put each tortilla on a microwavable plate or even a paper towel. Arrange cheese slices on top of the tortillas. Add a little salsa for those who like it. Cover the cheese on each with another tortilla or leave the quesadillas open-face. Microwave each quesadilla until the cheese melts (30 seconds to one minute). Cut into strips or wedges and enjoy. Look for more easy recipes for tasty, kid-friendly food in Chapter 10 of *The New Complete Babysitter's Handbook* by Carol Barkin and Elizabeth James, who contributed this recipe.

CHICKEN STRIPS to go
with "Ballad of the Boneless Chicken" in *New Kid on the Block* by Jack Prelutsky, illustrated by James Stevenson, Greenwillow: ISBN 0688022715 (hc).

■ These tasty boneless strips are just what little poets need.

Ingredients
6 boneless chicken breasts sliced into finger-sized strips
1/4 cup olive oil
1 sleeve Ritz crackers
1/2 cup Parmesan cheese
1/4 teaspoon garlic powder

Dipster Dip
Hidden Valley Ranch salad dressing
1 teaspoon dried dill
2 tablespoons dill pickle relish

Directions
After you cut the chicken breasts into strips, dump them in a big bowl with the oil, and moosh it around with your hands until the chicken fingers are all coated with oil. Crush the Ritz crackers however suits your mood best, then combine Ritz remnants with cheese and garlic powder in a bowl. Dip each chicken finger in the cracker mixture and coat it with crumbs (or as Amelia Bedelia would say, "Dress it"). Place on cookie sheet and bake for about 30 minutes until browned. Serve with Dipster Dip: Hidden Valley Ranch salad dressing mixed with dried dill and dill pickle chopped up into microscopic pieces.

DIATONIC DITTYMUNCH EDIBLE OPERA STICKS
from *New Kid on the Block* by Jack Prelutsky, illustrated by James Stevenson, Greenwillow: ISBN 0688022715 (hc).

■ While eating these "batons," you could conduct a whole orchestra with Prelutsky's lyrical verses, including the one about "Euphonica Jarre with her voice most bizarre."

Ingredients
1 bag small pretzel sticks (not the giant ones)
1 package cheese sticks
2 cans Vienna sausages
black olives
baby gherkin pickles

Directions
On pretzel sticks, layer 1/2-inch pieces of cheese sticks, 1/2-inch pieces of the Vienna sausages, black olives, and 1/2-inch pickle pieces. Serve while listening to opera.

DORA DILLER'S EDIBLE CATERPILLARS to go with *New Kid on the Block* by Jack Prelutsky, illustrated by James Stevenson, Greenwillow: ISBN 0688022715 (hc).

■ You could also use this with other caterpillar books such *The Very Hungry Caterpillar* by Eric Carle, Putnam: ISBN 0399208534.

Ingredients
12 cheese sticks
peanut butter
sprouts
black olive slices

Directions
Cut cheese sticks in half lengthwise. Slather the round part with peanut butter, then attach sprouts to be the "hair" of the caterpillar. Use two olive slices for eyes. Place 12 olive slice halves along each side of the "caterpillar," and point them backward to look like the feet of the caterpillar.

JELLYFISH STEW to go with *New Kid on the Block* by Jack Prelutsky, illustrated by James Stevenson, Greenwillow: ISBN 0688022715 (hc).

■ These yucky-looking little jellyfish treats are yummy and easy to make.

Ingredients
2 packages green Jell-O®
1 box Nilla® wafers (any flavor; your choice)

Other
round bowl to use as a mold

Directions
Mix Jell-O according to package directions. Pour into bowl to mold. When it is set, use a knife to make various slits in the "big jellyfish." Insert Nilla wafers into the slits as "little jellyfish."

UNDERWATER WIBBLES CHEESE EXTRAVAGANZA

to go with *New Kid on the Block* by Jack Prelutsky, illustrated by James Stevenson, Greenwillow: ISBN 0688022715 (hc).

■ The book features a poem all about the gazillion different kinds of cheese that the Underwater Wibbles love, so set this up as a cheese-tasting experience. Most supermarkets have a variety of exotic cheeses available. If you have access to a health food store or a gourmet delicatessen, you might be able to find several other kinds of cheese.

Ingredients
(use 4 ounces of each of the following:)

cheddar cheese	Gouda cheese
Gorgonzola cheese	provolone cheese
Muenster cheese	Camembert cheese
feta cheese	mozzarella cheese
Brie cheese	Appenzeller cheese

Directions
Cut cheese into small dice-sized cubes. Put each kind of cheese on a separate paper plate. Write on the plate what kind of cheese it is. Let students taste each kind of "Wibbles" with a toothpick, or if you can find them, use little hors d'oeuvre forks like tridents. Neptune was the God of the Sea, and a trident was his gift from the Titan Vulcan. When he banged it on the ocean floor, earthquakes and tidal waves erupted just like Underwater Wibbles would love.

NIGHT SHIFT DADDY APPLE PIE to go with

Night Shift Daddy by Eileen Spinelli, illustrations by Melissa Iwai, Hyperion: ISBN 0786804955 (hc).

■ A father shares his milk and apple pie with his daughter before he heads to work as a night janitor.

Ingredients

5 cups sliced apples	2 tablespoons butter
2/3 cup sugar	3 tablespoons quick-cooking
1/3 cup light brown sugar, packed	tapioca
1 teaspoon ground cinnamon	1/4 teaspoon ground all
1/4 teaspoon ground nutmeg	spice
1/4 teaspoon salt	1 package premade pie
1 tablespoon lemon juice	crusts (two per package)

Directions
Mix the first 10 ingredients together and spoon into a 9-inch pastry-lined pie pan. Top with a full crust. Cut slits in the top crust to let the steam escape. Bake at 425°F for 20 minutes, then at 375°F for 40 minutes.

NOAH'S RAINBOW COOKIES to go with

Noah's Ark by Peter Spier, Yearling: ISBN 0440406935 (pbk).

■ Making little edible rainbows to remember the Great Flood's end can be also combined with *The Rainbow Goblins* by Ul De Rico, Thames & Hudson: ISBN 0500277591, or other books about the visible spectrum and prisms.

Ingredients

1 cup soft margarine
1 1/2 cups sugar
2 eggs
1 teaspoon vanilla
3 cups flour
1/2 teaspoon baking soda
1/2 teaspoon salt
food coloring (four colors)

Directions

Group 1: Cream together margarine, sugar, eggs, and vanilla.

Group 2: Mix together flour, baking soda, and salt.

Group 3: Blend flour mixture (from Group 2) into margarine mixture (from Group 1).

Group 4: Divide the finished dough into four parts.

Group 5: Add a few drops of a different color food color to each of the four parts and mix well by kneading color into cookie dough.

Group 6: On wax paper, pat each dough section into a 4-inch-wide strip (one hand wide, one finger thick, one cubit long).

Group 7: Stack the strips and refrigerate overnight. Next day, slice into 1/4-inch slices, make it arch, and put on cookie sheet.

Group 8: Bake at 350°F for seven minutes.

FALL APPLE CRISP to go

with *Oats and Wild Apples* by Frank Asch, Puffin: ISBN 0823406776 (hc).

■ Baby animals love oats and wild apples—students will too.

Ingredients
12 baking apples (peeled, cored, and sliced)
1 cup brown sugar
1/2 cup flour
1/2 cup rolled oats
1 teaspoon cinnamon
1 teaspoon nutmeg
1 stick butter

Directions
Put apples and sugar into buttered 8-inch square cake pan. Mix together flour, rolled oats, cinnamon, nutmeg, and butter. Cut together with a fork until it's crumbly, then sprinkle over apples. Bake at 350°F about an hour.

BARE CUPBOARD DOGGY BONES to go

with *Old Mother Hubbard and Her Wonderful Dog* by James Marshall, Farrar, Straus, and Giroux: ISBN 0374356211 (hc), Sunburst: 0374456119 (pbk).

■ These are real dog biscuits for kids or dogs, unlike the dog "cookies" in the Clifford recipe.

Ingredients
2 1/2 cups whole wheat flour
1/2 cup powdered dry milk
1/2 teaspoon salt
1 teaspoon garlic powder
1/2 teaspoon onion powder
2 teaspoons brown sugar
1 teaspoon granulated beef bouillon
6 tablespoons meat drippings
1 egg, beaten
1/2 cup ice water

Directions
Combine flour, milk, salt, onion and garlic powder, sugar, and bouillon. Cut in drippings until mixture looks like cornmeal. Mix in egg. Add just enough ice water to make mixture form a ball. Pat dough to a 1/2-inch thickness and cut into doggy-bone shapes. Place on a lightly greased cookie sheet, and bake at 350°F for about 25 minutes.

MARSHMALLOW MOUTONS to go with
One Small Lost Sheep
by Claudia Mills,
illustrated by Walter Lyon
Krudop, Farrar, Straus,
and Giroux: ISBN
0374356491 (hc).

■ On a wintry night in Bethlehem, Benjamin loses his beloved lamb and later finds her in the most miraculous place of all. Children can make their own flock of edible marshmallow sheep. This recipe can also be used with many other sheep books.

Ingredients
1 bag of large marshmallows
1 bag of small marshmallows
1 package of small black gum drops

Other
toothpicks

Directions
Form sheep body by sticking two large marshmallows on a toothpick. Use a small marshmallow for the tail. For the legs, break toothpicks in half; use two small marshmallows for each leg. If desired, use half of a gumdrop instead of the second small marshmallow to form a hoof. For the head, break another toothpick and use half of a large marshmallow. Complete the sheep with two small marshmallows for ears, then make a whole flock! Contributed by Claudia Mills.

ORANGE BOATS to go with *The Owl and the Pussycat* by Edward Lear, illustrated by Jan Brett, Philomel: ISBN 0399231935 (hc), PaperStar: 0698113675,

■ The Owl and the Pussycat went to sea in a beautiful "pea-green boat," which is what these turn into after you cut the oranges into quarters.

Ingredients

6 navel oranges, cut in half and hollowed out
2 packages green Jell-O®
12 slices white American cheese

Other
toothpicks

Directions

Pull the insides out of halved navel oranges, while trying to keep the peels intact. Fill each "boat" with green Jell-O, which has been made with only half the water called for in the package directions. Refrigerate the "boats," probably overnight. When you're ready to serve them, cut each half in half with a wet knife and add a sail made from a slice of white American cheese on a toothpick or pretzel stick (it's much harder to keep the piece of cheese intact on the pretzel stick as it tends to split the cheese). Kids like to eat the stiff Jell-O right out of the orange rinds.

TROPICAL CAKE to go with Jan Brett's *The Owl and the Pussycat* by Edward Lear, Philomel: ISBN 0399231935 (hc), PaperStar: 0698113675 (pbk), Putnam: 0399329350 (lb).

■ This tasty cake is chockfull of tropical ingredients. You could mix it with a runcible spoon, if you've got one handy.

Ingredients

1 yellow cake mix
1 cup vegetable oil
4 eggs
1 small can mandarin oranges, juice and all

Tropical Topping

1 can crushed pineapple, drained
1 package instant vanilla pudding mix
1 9-ounce container Cool Whip®

Directions

Mix cake ingredients in a large bowl. Beat together well, pour into a greased and floured pan, bake at 350°F for 35 minutes or until toothpick inserted in middle comes out clean. Let cool. Mix together ingredients for Tropical Topping, then slather on cooled cake.

EDIBLE EYEBALLS

to go with *Parts* by
Tedd Arnold, Dial: ISBN
0803720408 (hc),
0803720416 (lb).

■ Youngsters love this highly gross and disgusting book, and it's great to booktalk. In the story, a boy is afraid he is falling apart and his eyeballs will fall out. These edible eyeballs look like the ones in the book.

Ingredients
2 pounds ground turkey or chicken
2 eggs
1 cup bread crumbs
1 package turkey gravy mix
24 green olives with pimento in the middle
2 cups mashed potatoes (you could do with instant potatoes)

Directions
Moosh ground meat, eggs, bread crumbs and gravy mix together with clean hands and make eyeball-sized meatballs. Insert a green olive with pimento in the middle right into the "eyeball" where the iris would be. Bake these on a cookie sheet at 350°F about an hour, until they are rubbery, or at least not soft any more. Serve on a "bed" of mashed potatoes to look like the white of the eyes. Pretty disgusting, huh?

SUPERIOR LOGS to go

with *Paul Bunyan* by
Steven Kellogg, William
Morrow: ISBN
0688058000 (pbk),
0688038506 (lb).

■ After you make these "logs," you can line them up like a logjam and eat them using wooden "pikes" (skewers).

Ingredients
12 zucchinis
2 pounds ground turkey
1 package meatloaf seasoning mix

Other
wooden skewers (optional)

Directions
Hollow out 12 halved zucchinis with a melon baller. Stuff with turkey meatball mix made from two pounds ground turkey mixed with meatloaf seasoning mix. Reassemble zucchini "logs," and line up like a logjam on a broiler pan (so the turkey juice can run out and not make the zucchinis soggy). Bake at 375° about an hour until turkey is done.

MUNCHY BAD RABBIT'S CARROT SALAD to go
with *Peter Rabbit* by Beatrix Potter, Penguin: ISBN 0140860169 (hc), or try the stand-up storybook *Peter Rabbit and Friends*, Warne: 0723243433 (hc).

■ Peter Rabbit's illicit search for carrots in dangerous Mr. MacGregor's garden would have been obviated by this snack.

Ingredients
24 carrots
12 handfuls raisins
mayonnaise
lettuce leaves

Directions
Shred carrots in food processor (two carrots per child is a good start). Mix shredded carrot, raisins, and mayonnaise to taste in a bowl. Make a tasty, little pile of carrot salad on a nice, soporific lettuce leaf.

ENGLISH MUFFIN PIZZAS to go with *Pete's a Pizza* by William Steig, HarperCollins: ISBN 0062051571 (hc).

■ Pete's dad makes him a pizza and then sends him out to play when the rain ends. Kids can make these pizzas themselves—rain or shine.

Ingredients
12 English muffin halves
2 jars Pizza Quick® sauce
2 cups shredded mozzarella
oregano to sprinkle

Directions
Lay English muffin half on firm surface and smoonch it flat by leaning on it with the palm of your hand. Toast it. Put on two tablespoons of pizza sauce. Sprinkle with mozzarella (try to keep cheese in the middle). Put two shakes of oregano on top. Bake on cookie sheet at 350°F until cheese melts.

FEAST to go with *Picnic Farm* by Christine Morton, Holiday House: ISBN 0823413322 (lb).

■ This tidy, little casserole picnic dish will look just like the treat in the story if you serve it on a red, checkered tablecloth

Ingredients
1 loaf French bread slices
1 dozen eggs
1 cup milk
1 jar bacon bits
12 slices Swiss cheese
12 slices American cheese

Directions
In two 9x11 greased baking pans, put slices of French bread to cover the bottom. In a separate bowl, scramble the eggs and milk. Pour over bread. Add a sprinkling of bacon bit. Add a layer of Swiss cheese, then add a layer of American cheese. Refrigerate overnight. Bake at 350°F for an hour. Cut into squares, and serve on a paper plate with picnic tablecloth.

PIGGIE PIE to go with the *Piggie Pie* by Margie Palatini, illustrated by Howard Fine, Houghton Mifflin: ISBN 0395716918 (hc), Clarion: 0395866189 (pbk).

■ The witch has a hard time finding those devious little piggies to put in her pic because they disguise themselves so well.

Ingredients
1 can chicken meat
1 small can chicken broth
1 onion, chopped
2 stalks celery, sliced
3 carrots, sliced
1 potato, cubed
1 box frozen string beans, thawed
1 loaf French bread, sliced

Directions
Combine and cook all ingredients except bread in a crock-pot for three hours. Serve in bowls with a piece of French bread on the bottom to soak up the "piggie" juices.

PAT'S PIZZA to go with
Pizza Pat by Rita Golden
Gelman illustrated by
Will Terry, Random House:
ISBN 067989134X (pbk),
0679991344 (lb);
Pizza Party! by Grace
MacCarone, Scholastic:
0590475630 (pbk); or
*A Pizza the Size of the
Sun* by Jack Prelutsky,
illustrated by James
Stevenson, Greenwillow:
0688132359 (hc).

■ Jack Prelutsky says, "[Pizza] should include oceans of sauce, mountains of cheese, acres of peppers, pimentos, and peas; mushrooms, tomatoes, and sausage galore, and all the olives you can find." Making little pizzas from biscuits is a great shortcut for children. The books are easy readers, and students could write their own recipe and story after this activity.

Ingredients
2 cans refrigerator biscuits
1 jar Pizza Quick® sauce
grated mozzarella cheese
oregano or Italian seasoning

Directions
Pat the biscuits to flatten them a little, top with two tablespoons Pizza Quick sauce, a little cheese, some spices, and bake on a cookie sheet at 350°F for about 15 minutes until rims are brown.

BEDOUIN DROMEDARY CAMEL CHEESE to go with
Pizza the Size of the Sun by Jack Prelutsky, illustrated by James Stevenson, Greenwillow: ISBN 0688132359 (hc), 0688132367 (lb).

■ In the desert, nomads often put camel milk in "canteens" made from camel stomachs. The sloshing and heat turn the milk to a sort of cottage cheese. No camel stomachs are required for this—unless you have some handy.

Ingredients
2 quarts heavy whipping cream
4 rennet tablets
4 tablespoons water
honey
figs and dates, cut into small pieces
nuts (optional)

Other
cheesecloth
colander

Directions
Dissolve rennet tablets in 4 tablespoons water. In a large bowl, mix the rennet mixture into the cream, stir to the count of 12. Let it sit for about 20 minutes. This clabbers it. Cut with bamboo skewers, table knives, or Saracen swords if you have some handy. Line a colander with cheese cloth. Pour the mixture into the colander. Now comes the authentic part. Let it drip for about ten minutes, then firmly tie the cheesecloth closed with a string, and jog it around and around and around the playground to drive out the whey (the juice). Perhaps you want to set up a "camel track," and have each kid carry the cheese one lap around. This simulates it being jogged around by the camel in the desert. After it's well drained, add honey, pieces of figs and dates, and nuts if you want, or any other sort of Bedouin food that comes to mind. Mix well and serve with spoons.

LEMON WAITING WAFFLES to go with

Poetry Is My Underwear
by April Halprin Wayland,
Knopf: ISBN 0375801588
(hc), 0375901582 (lb).

■ April Wayland tells how when she was a teen, one of her friends found her poetry journal that held all her deepest concerns about the world, war, and boys. April recalls, "I was mortified because letting people read my poetry was like lifting up my skirt and letting them see my underwear." In the collection is a poem called "Waiting for Waffles," which is about waiting. . . and writing . . . and waffles. These waffles may or may not assuage mortification, but they sure are tasty.

Ingredients
4 eggs separated
3 tablespoons honey
1 cup milk
2 teaspoons fresh lemon juice
2 tablespoons grated lemon zest
1/4 cup butter, melted and cooled
1 cup flour

Directions
In a medium bowl, beat egg yolks with honey. Blend in the lemon juice, lemon zest, and butter, beating well. Blend in the milk and flour alternately. Beat egg whites until stiff and fold into batter. Bake in prepared waffle iron until golden brown. Makes four large waffles. Cut into segments. Contributed by April Halprin Wayland.

ANZAC BISCUITS AND RELATED AUSSIE TREATS

to go with *Possum Magic* by Mem Fox, illustrated by Julie Vivas, Harcourt: ISBN 0152005722 (hc), 0152632247 (pbk).

■ In the story, different Australian foods are eaten to try to make the little possum visible again. This is a Down Under feast.

Ingredients
1 cup rolled oats
3/4 cup coconut shredded
3/4 cup flour
1/2 cup butter
1 teaspoon honey
3 teaspoons boiling water
1 1/2 teaspoon baking soda

Directions
Put oats, coconut, flour, and sugar into a large bowl and mix. Melt butter and honey together in a separate bowl. Boil water. Pour boiling water over the baking soda and stir to dissolve. Add this to the butter mixture. Mix the butter mixture with the dry mixture until it forms a sticky batter. Drop batter by teaspoonfuls about 2 inches apart on a greased baking sheet. Bake at 300˚F for about 10 minutes until browned.

Ingredients for the rest of the Feast
Vegemite (usually available in health food stores)
white bread (toasted) for sandwiches, or you could use Melba toast
Premade meringue cups
Whipped cream or Cool Whip®
Fresh or frozen thawed fruit
sponge cake cut into Twinkie®-sized pieces
Hershey's chocolate sauce
shredded coconut

Directions
Spread Vegemite very thin on white bread slices. To make Pavlova, fill a meringue shell with whipped cream or Cool Whip and fresh fruit of any kind. To make Lamington, dip pieces of sponge cake into thin chocolate sauce and then roll them in coconut so that they look like little, white lambs with brown skin.

PRETZEL'S SNACKS to go

with *Pretzel* by Margret Rey, illustrations by H. A. Rey, Houghton Mifflin: ISBN 0395837375 (hc), 0395837332 (pbk).

■ Pretzel is a v-e-r-y long wiener dog who manages to rescue his sweetie pie from a very deep hole because of his length. Obviously, dachshunds don't like the idea of hot dogs on a bun, so this is Pretzel's favorite long skinny snack.

Ingredients
12 bananas
12 hot dog rolls
peanut butter
marshmallow fluff

Directions
Spread peanut butter on insides of top and bottom of hot dog roll. Now spread some marshmallow fluff on the peanut butter. Now insert a peeled banana so it looks like a hot dog.

SECRET GREEN STUFF

to go with *Pueblo and Navajo Indian Life Today*, written and illustrated by Kris Hotvedt, Sunstone Press: ISBN 0865342040 (pbk).

■ This treat is made by the author's friend, Erly Crazy Horse, for feast days at Cochiti (pronounced "COE-chitty") Pueblo in New Mexico. Everyone loves it, even the coyotes and critters.

Ingredients
1 package instant pistachio pudding
1 8-ounce container Cool Whip®
1 14-ounce can pineapple chunks with juice
1 cup miniature marshmallows
1/2 cup chopped nuts, optional

Directions
Put dry pudding in a big bowl. Drain the pineapple and save the juice. Set the pineapple chunks aside to use later. Add the juice to the pudding in the big bowl. Blend with a wire whisk or use a blender on low speed. Gradually mix in the Cool Whip, blending in the whole container. Fold in the miniature marshmallows. Add the pineapple chunks and stir until all the pineapple juice is mixed in. After it is all mixed up, stir in the nuts if you want to add them and mix again. Refrigerate for at least an hour. Guard the refrigerator from coyotes and critters. After an hour, you can eat and enjoy the Green Stuff. Contributed by Kris Hotvedt.

EASY PUMPKIN CAKE to

go with *Pumpkin Pumpkin* by Jeanne Titherington, William Morrow: ISBN 0688056954 (hc), 0688099300 (pbk); *The Pumpkin Patch* by Elizabeth King, Econo-Clad: 0613005201 (hc), Puffin: 014055968X (pbk), Dutton: 0525446400 (lb); or *Too Many Pumpkins* by Linda White, illustrated by Megan Lloyd, Holiday House: 0823413209 (pbk) 0823412458 (lb).

■ Kids often visit a pumpkin patch in the fall, and could easily use fresh pumpkin pulp to make this recipe. The first two suggested titles are "sagas" of a pumpkin from seed to dessert. In Linda White's book, an old lady makes every imaginable kind of pumpkin food to get rid of her bounty.

Ingredients
1 package spice cake mix
1 small can pumpkin pie filling
1 egg
2 tablespoons milk

Icing
strawberry-flavored cream cheese

Directions
Mix all cake ingredients together in a food processor. Divide into paper-lined muffin tin and bake at 350°F for 20 minutes. Let cool, then add cream cheese icing.

PRETZEL RAFTS ON BLUE FRUIT LEATHER RIVERS

to go with *The Raft* by Jim Lamarche, HarperCollins: ISBN 0688139779 (hc).

■ Sailing down a summer river on an old-fashioned log raft, merging with nature can be vicariously recreated in this edible "raft" on edible "water."

Ingredients
pretzel sticks (any size)
honey
Monterey Jack cheese
blue fruit roll-ups or fruit leather

Directions
This recipe is a bit labor-intensive and is more for looking at than eating, but there will be some breakage of pretzels that the kids can eat and, of course, the sticky hands from honey, so children will have to keep licking their fingers. To make one raft, it takes 12 pretzel sticks and a lot of honey to make them cohere. Build the raft on two pretzel sticks as "beams." Cut a thick slice of cheese in the shape of a sail and add (it should be thick enough to stand up by itself on the pretzel raft). Serve on a "river" of blue fruit leather.

RAGGEDY ANDY'S TAFFY

to go with *The Raggedy Andy Stories* by Johnny Gruelle, Simon & Schuster: ISBN 0027375862 (hc).

■ Andy says: "Take sugar and water and butter and a little vinegar, and put it all on the stove to cook. When it has cooked until it strings way out when you dip some up in a spoon, or gets hard when you drop some of it in a cup of water, then it is candy. Then it must be placed upon buttered plates until it has cooled a little, and then each one takes some of the candy and pulls and pulls until it gets real white."

Ingredients

2 cups sugar
1 cup light Karo syrup
1 cup water
1 1/2 teaspoons salt
2 tablespoons butter
1/4 teaspoon peppermint extract
food color (optional)
butter (for hands)

Directions

Butter a 9x14x2-inch baking dish and set aside. Butter the sides of a two-quart saucepan. Combine the sugar, syrup, water, and salt in the saucepan. Cook over medium heat, stirring consistently until it boils. Then clip a candy thermometer to the side of the pan, and boil without stirring until it comes to 265˚F (hard-ball stage), usually about 40 minutes. Remove pan from heat. Remove thermometer. Stir in butter, extract, coloring. Pour into prepared pan. Cool one-half hour. Lightly butter hands, then handle and mold candy into little shapes.

EASY BLENDER APPLESAUCE to go with
Rain Makes Applesauce by Julian Scheer, illustrated by Marvin Bilecki, Holiday House: ISBN 0823400913 (hc).

■ The wonderful rhythm of this poem-story can be interspersed with blender noises while the students chant the refrain. You could also use the recipe with any apple story, such as *Johnny Appleseed* by Steven Kellogg, William Morrow: ISBN 0688064175 (hc).

Ingredients
12 apples (one per child)
2 tablespoons water (to "rain" on the applesauce)
1 tablespoon honey

Other
blender
paper cups

Directions
Peel and quarter apples. Remove all seeds. Fill blender half-full with apple pieces. Add water and honey. Blend until smooth. Continue until all apples are used. After you blend each batch, pour applesauce into paper cups.

RAINBABIES IN A DRAWER to go with *The Rainbabies* by Laura Krauss Melmed, illustrated by Jim LaMarche, Lothrop Lee and Shepard: ISBN 0688107559 (hc).

■ These "rainbabies" are so cute you could eat them—as a matter of fact, you DO.

Ingredients
12 precooked link sausages
12 pieces white bread
12 slices American cheese
12 cherry tomatoes
green bell pepper

Directions
In a long, 13x8x2-inch baking dish, evenly lay out sausages (the babies), each on a "bed" of a bread slice. Cover with cheese slice "blankets," leaving room for the "heads," which are cherry tomatoes. Add a little blanket satin strip made of very thin slices of green pepper. Nuke until cheese melts but does not bubble. Let cool before serving because the sausages get hot.

COLOR FEAST to go with *The Rainbow Goblins* by Ul De Rico, Thames & Hudson: ISBN 0500277591 (hc).

■ Celebrate the survival of color in the world—in spite of the goblins' evil plan to suck all the red, green, yellow, and orange away forever.

Ingredients

papaya
dried apricot
butternut squash
navel orange
carrot
broccoli florets
peas (fresh or frozen)
string beans (fresh or canned)
honeydew melon
grapes (green and purple)
peach
kiwi
lemon
corn
grapefruit
radish
watermelon

Directions

On paper plates have youngsters each write the following phrases: "Orange Is . . .," "Green Is . . .," "Yellow Is . . .," and "Red Is . . .." and so on (see the following list).

ORANGE IS . . . a papaya
ORANGE IS . . . an apricot (dried or canned)
ORANGE IS . . . a butternut squash
ORANGE IS . . . an orange
ORANGE IS . . . a carrot
GREEN IS . . . broccoli
GREEN IS . . . peas
GREEN IS . . . string beans
GREEN IS . . . honeydew melon
GREEN IS . . . kiwi fruit
GREEN IS . . . a grape
YELLOW IS. . . peaches
YELLOW IS . . . grapefruit
YELLOW IS . . . a lemon
YELLOW IS . . . corn
RED IS . . . a strawberry
RED IS . . . a grape
RED IS . . . a radish
RED IS . . . a tomato
RED IS . . . watermelon

Cut up pieces of the listed foods and put 12 pieces on each plate. Give each student an empty paper plate to use for his or her feasting pleasure and have them collect one piece of each treat. See if children can identify the foods by taste or looks as they settle in for a colorful snack.

RAINBOW COOKIES to go
with *The Rainbow Goblins*
by Ul De Rico, Thames &
Hudson: ISBN
0500277591 (hc).

■ The Rainbow Goblins try to eat up all the colors but are thwarted. These cookies should be brightly colored to celebrate the defeat of the goblins and the return of color to the world.

Ingredients

1 cup soft margarine
   or butter
1 1/2 cup sugar
2 eggs
1 teaspoon vanilla

3 cups flour
1/2 teaspoon baking soda
1/2 teaspoon salt
food coloring (red, yellow, blue, green)

Directions

Mix butter, sugar, eggs, and vanilla together. In a separate bowl, mix flour, soda, salt. Blend dry mixture into wet mixture until dough forms. Divide dough into four parts. Generously add one color to each part, moosh together well by hand. Pat dough into fat little strips. Push strips together side by side on wax paper to form a long, striped dough "bar." Refrigerate overnight. Cut into 1/4-inch slices and mold each slice into an arch (a rainbow). Bake at 350°F for seven minutes.

ANGEL HAIR PASTA
to go with *Rapunzel* by
Paul O. Zelinsky, Dutton:
ISBN 0525456074 (hc).

■ This could be used with any *Rapunzel* version you have on hand. It looks terrific, and children will enjoy it.

Ingredients

1 package angel hair pasta
water to cook pasta
6 zucchinis

12 olives
Parmesan cheese topping
1 jar pimentos

Directions

Cook one package angel hair pasta to al dente, keeping noodles in a long, straight line. This is best accomplished by cooking the pasta in a frying pan. Give each child three long bunches of noodles (lay out straight on a piece of wax paper or paper plates to braid). Lay cooked zucchini halves on plate to be the "towers" and nuke for about seven minutes to cook through. Cut out a little square "window" near the top third of the zucchini, add an olive "face" in the window, and insert the angel hair braid. Sprinkle braid with Parmesan cheese. Add a red "ribbon," a piece of pimento, to the bottom of the braid.

RECHENKA'S EGGS to go

with *Rechenka's Eggs* by Patricia Polacco, Putnam: ISBN 0399215018 (hc).

■ Pysanka is an ancient Ukrainian egg-decorating method that uses ink and a variety of techniques and tools. It likely would be too complicated for children. This recipe offers a more child-friendly version.

Ingredients
12 blown eggs
canning wax

Other
pins
Magic Markers™
blow dryer
paper towels or newspaper

Directions
To blow eggs, prick a hole the size of a pea in the large end of the egg. Prick a hole the size of a sesame seed in the small end of the egg. Hold the egg over a bowl. Blow very hard in the small hole and the white and yolk will run out of the large hole. You end up with a nice, hollow egg! Melt canning wax in a bowl in the microwave. While it's still liquid, roll each blown egg in the wax until it is coated. Let wax dry. Incise designs (*see designs in Polacco's book*) with a pin or dead ballpoint pen for the first color application. With Magic Marker™, apply color to the incised areas. Etch second design, and carefully apply the second color on those lines. If you are really careful, you can incise a third set of designs and apply color to those as well. When all the colors are dry, you can melt the wax with a blow dryer, letting the drips fall on paper towels. What you end up with is a lovely delicately decorated Pysanka-style egg.

CHICKEN FEED to go with *Rosie's Walk* by Pat Hutchins, Simon & Schuster: ISBN 0027458504 (hc), Aladdin: 0020437501 (pbk), Little Simon: 0689822316 (board book).

■ As Rosie crosses the barnyard picking up treats, students could have plenty of fun snacking on this mixture from newspaper on the floor—no hands allowed. Or you could make it easy and let them eat it out of a paper cup.

Ingredients
1 cup Cheerios®
1 cup Rice Chex® cereal
1 cup Wheat Chex® cereal
1 cup any kind of shelled peanuts
1 cup sunflower seed kernels
1 cup raisins
1 cup M&M's

Directions
Mix all ingredients together in a huge bowl or feed bucket (more authentic). Divide up into individual cups. As a "100th Day of School" treat, kids could count out 100 of each ingredient to add to the mix and read *Miss Bindergarten Celebrates the 100th Day* by Joseph Slate, illustrated by Ashley Wolff, Dutton Books: ISBN 0525460004 (hc).

ROTTEN RALPH'S KITTY LITTER CAKE TREAT to go

with *Rotten Ralph* by Jack Gantos and Nicole Rubel, Houghton Mifflin: ISBN 0395242762 (hc), 0685023079 (pbk).

■ Rotten Ralph is without doubt the worst cat on the planet. This would be his idea of a great snack.

Ingredients

1 box white cake mix
1 box spice cake mix
1 package vanilla pudding and enough milk to prepare it (or premade vanilla pudding)
1 package vanilla sandwich cookies
green food coloring
4 or 5 big Tootsie Roll® candies
1 new litter box
1 new litter scoop

Directions

Prepare each cake mix separately, according to directions. Crush vanilla cookies in a blender or by hand in a Ziploc bag until they become "kitty litter" sized pieces. Mix about one-fourth of the cookie crumbs with enough green food coloring for a nice "chlorophyll" look. Prepare vanilla pudding. Crumble both cakes together into a new (unused) regular-size cat litter box. Heap into creative piles. Warm the Tootsie Rolls in the microwave, 10 seconds at a time so they get soft and malleable. Shape them into . . . well, you know . . . what litter packages refer to as "solid waste." Bury them appropriately in the "litter." Spread the pudding over the litter following the contours of the surface. Mix the green cookie crumbs with the plain crumbs so the result looks like "litter green." Sprinkle this over the surface of the cake. Keep refrigerated, and serve with the new litter scoop. Contributed by Bob Vardeman.

THREE MEN IN A TUB

to go with *Rub a Dub Dub* by Kin Eagle, Whispering Coyote Press: ISBN 1580890083 (bd).

■ These cute, little tubs with stand-up "guys" in them are great fun to make and eat.

Ingredients
6 baked potatoes, halved with the insides scooped out and mashed
6 tablespoons milk (for mashing potatoes)
3 cans SPAM® canned luncheon meat
12 slices turkey lunchmeat
12 lunchmeat ham slices
6 white breadsticks, sliced and hollowed out a little

Directions
For the "three men," cut the contents of each can of SPAM into 12 sticks. Make 12 of the "men" with SPAM wrapped in turkey slices, and 12 "men" with SPAM wrapped in ham slices. Make "baker men" by hollowing out breadsticks cut in half to make 12 fat, little men and inserting a slice of SPAM. Put all of the "men" in the "boat" made from the baked potato and surround them with the mashed potatoes to make them stand. They can be warmed in the microwave or a 350°F oven.

HOMEMADE BUTTER

to go with *Sam and the Tigers* by Julius Lester, illustrated by Jerry Pinkney, Dial: ISBN 0803720289 (hc), 0803720297 (lb).

■ The tigers chase each other round and round until they turn into butter, which Sam puts on his pancakes. This is a much less dangerous way to get homemade butter. You could also use the recipe with *The Story of Little Babaji* by Helen Bannerman, illustrated by Fred Marcellino, HarperCollins: ISBN 0062050648.

Ingredients
1 quart heavy cream
12 empty baby-food-size jars with lids that fit tightly

Directions
Fill each jar halfway with cream. Put the lid on TIGHTLY. Shake and shake and shake steadily for about 15 minutes. Singing a song (or reading a book) helps pass the time. After the butter has formed, you can add salt or just use it as is on pancakes or bread.

SUPER FRITTATA to go with *Scrambled Eggs Super* by Dr. Seuss, Random House: ISBN 0394800850 (hc).

■ This casserole can be tinkered with if you want to add or subtract ingredients—it's a pretty forgiving recipe. Most kids will enjoy it because after it comes out of the oven, you can cut it and they won't recognize it as scrambled eggs.

Ingredients
12 eggs
1/2 pound bacon
1 zucchini
1 red bell pepper
1 green bell pepper
1/2 cup Monterey Jack cheese
1 bunch green onions
3 tablespoons butter

Directions
Crack and whip eggs. Cut up bacon into small slices then microwave on paper towels or fry. Cut zucchini, cored and seeded red and green peppers, and cheese into very thin, very small pieces. Also cut green onions into tiny pieces for color. Children usually hate onions, so you can use just the tops for color, or even omit the onions altogether. In a large frying pan, heat butter till melted but not browned. Add eggs, then add chopped vegetables in even layers. Bake in 350°F oven for about an hour, or nuke for about 12 minutes on 50% in microwave (don't nuke eggs on high or they turn into a rubbery inedible substance like rubber tires). Cut into tidy little squares after it cools down a bit.

FOUR AND TWENTY BLACKBIRDS BAKED IN A PIE to go with *Sing a Song of Sixpence* by Pam Adams, Childs Play International: ISBN 0859536270 (pbk).

■ These little pocket-full-of-rye pies have blackbirds aplenty in them. Counting out the "four and twenty" ought to make them even more fun.

Ingredients
2 packages ready-made pie crust
1 large can apple pie filling
raisins

Directions
In a 12-hole muffin tin, line each cup with a circle of ready-made pie dough that you've cut into a circle about twice as big as the hole in the muffin tin (this is a good opportunity for measuring using non-ruler techniques—try using dental floss or a piece of thread). Bake until crispy in a moderate oven (350°F). Spoon three tablespoons canned apple pie filling into each baked pie crust. Have each child count out 24 raisins (these are the blackbirds) and add them to his or her little pie. Add one more spoonful of apple pie filling to cover the blackbirds. Add a top crust to each pie. Bake at 350°F for about 15 minutes, until tops are browned. Remove the pies with a big spoon, let cool, and then sing the song before you open up the pies. Protect your noses.

UGLY CHICKEN to go with *Sir Gawain and the Loathly Lady* by Selina Hastings, illustrated by Juan Wijngaard, Econo-Clad: ISBN 080859690X (hc), William Morrow: 0688070469 (pbk).

■ Sir Gawain was really "chicken" to marry the ugly old hag, but he was a knight of the Round Table and a man of his word.

Ingredients
3 precooked boneless chicken breasts, cut into 1/2-inch cubes
2 cans drained pineapple chunks
4 medium zucchini
2 red bell peppers cut into 1/2-inch square pieces

Other
wooden skewers

Directions
Spear alternating ingredients on wooden skewers (*see* **Lancelot's Meal on a Lance** *entry*), leaving about 2 inches at each end for handling. Lay on a paper plate and nuke for two minutes.

UNMELTABLE MASHED POTATO SNOWBALLS to

go with *The Snowy Day* by Ezra Jack Keats, Viking: ISBN 0140501827 (pbk), 0670654000 (lb).

■ In the tale, the snowball melts away to nothing. These substantial snowballs will not melt away but rather will stick to your ribs or your pocket—or whatever.

Ingredients

1 box instant mashed potato flakes
milk, warmed to body temperature
1 stick butter
1 container Parmesan cheese
ground pepper

Directions

Mix the instant potatoes with milk to the consistency of good "snowball snow." Melt butter in a large, flat bowl or on a plate with a "lip" (so the butter doesn't run totally away). Make a snowball using clean hands. Roll it in the butter. Put Parmesan cheese in a cookie sheet (to contain the mess) and grind a little fresh pepper into it (to represent dirt and rocks in the snowball). Roll your snowball covered with butter in the parmesan/pepper coating. Set aside for a few minutes while you read the book, then have a snowball snack.

FEARLESS FLYING HOT DOGS to go with the

poem from *Something Big Has Been Here* by Jack Prelutsky, illustrated by James Stevenson, Greenwillow: ISBN 0688064345 (hc).

■ The poem is stuffed with puns—help kids taste the delicious wordplay! As you eat these snacks and read the poem, you HAVE to groan and groan at the horrible tasteless puns. At least the snack is tasty!

Ingredients

12 hot dogs	ketchup
12 hot dog buns	1 can chili (no beans)
mustard	1 can sauerkraut
relish	

Directions

Boil or nuke the hot dogs. Put each on a bun. Put little bowls in the middle of the table with adequate spoons and knives so that kids can add the toppings as you come to them in the poem.

LITTLE, STINKY CHEESE MEN to go with *The Stinky Cheese Man and Other Fairly Stupid Tales* by Jon Scieszka, illustrated by Lane Smith, Viking: ISBN 067084487X (hc).

■ A Stinky Cheese Man with beady, little olive eyes rolls away with an evil grin on his face. These are miniature versions for each kid.

Ingredients
12 Laughing Cow or Bon Bell brand little wheels of cheese
pieces of nuked bacon for the mouths
capers for the eyes

Directions
Peel off the red wax wrappers and on each wheel put a little piece of bacon for the mouth and two capers for the eyes. If you use a toothpick to insert the ends of the bacon, the mouth will not fall off too fast. The capers will stay in the cheese if you made little holes with the toothpick and then stick the capers in. These little cheese men are not very stinky, but the kids will eat them.

STONE SOUP to go with *Stone Soup* by Marcia Brown, Atheneum/Simon & Schuster: ISBN 0684922967 (hc), 0689711034 (pbk).

■ The recipe depends on each villager contributing one small can of something to the soup. Let each child open a can and add it to the pot with the Magic Stone in it.

Ingredients
1 large clean stone (preferably with some "magic" in it)
1 small can corn
1 small can string beans
1 small can sliced carrots
1 package Lipton's chicken noodle soup dry mix
1 can boneless shredded chicken
1 small can black beans
1 small can hominy
1 small can diced or chopped tomatoes
1 small can mushrooms
1 small can beef broth

Directions
Place clean Magic Stone in the bottom of a BIG crock-pot. Let each child add one ingredient to the pot. Let soup boil for a few hours to blend the "magic" with the other ingredients.

YANGTZE RIVER MUD PIE CAKE to go with *The Story About Ping* by Marjorie Flack, illustrated by Kurt Weise, Viking: ISBN 0140502416 (pbk), 0670672238 (lb).

■ When Ping dives to the muddy river bottom and comes up with a fish, only the ring around his neck keeps him from swallowing it. This "mud pie cake" recipe could be embellished with some gummy fish or a few Pepperidge Farm Goldfish crackers to add to the *Ping* theme.

Ingredients
1 cup flour
1 cup whole wheat flour
4 tablespoons unsweetened
    cocoa
2 teaspoons baking soda

1/2 cup vegetable oil
1 cup honey
1 cup cold water
2 tablespoons vinegar
1 tablespoon vanilla

Other
chopsticks

Directions
In an 11x9-inch baking pan, mix all ingredients with chopsticks until most of the lumps are gone. Bake at 350°F for 30 minutes, or until a chopstick comes out clean.

OLD ITALIAN VARIANT SPAGHETTI to go with *Strega Nona* by Tomie dePaola, Simon & Schuster: ISBN 067166283X (hc), Aladdin: 0671666061 (pbk).

■ Big Anthony can't stop the spaghetti flow because he doesn't know the "secret" of blowing kisses at the Magic Pot. I wonder if he knew the secret about how to tell when the spaghetti is done cooking? How about you? Did you know that if you throw a strand of spaghetti at the ceiling and it sticks, it's done?

Ingredients
1 package of spaghetti
1 huge pot of water

salt to taste
spaghetti sauce in a jar (optional)

Directions
Cook spaghetti till it's done. Then pour spaghetti into a colander and bathe it in cold water to stop the cooking. You can nuke it to heat it up, with or without spaghetti sauce. Don't forget to blow kisses at the Magic Pot. Tomie dePaola tells a story about how when he won the Caldecott for *Strega Nona* and someone suggested that it was an "old Italian variant" of the *Little Pot That Wouldn't Stop*. dePaola's reply was, "I guess I'm the Old Italian Variant then."

OWL'S CAKE to go with *Summertime Song* by Irene Haas, Margaret McElderry : ISBN 0689505493 (hc)

■ The lovely little summer cake in the story is easy to make if you think like mice.

Ingredients
1 banana
whipped cream or Cool Whip®
little blue flowers or blue cake-decorating sprinkles

Other
birthday candles

Directions
Cut one banana into 12 round slices. Add a touch of whipped cream or a dollop of Cool Whip on top of each banana "cake" and add little blue flowers (cake-decorating shops have them) to make it look like the blueberries on the teeny-tiny cake. You can also sprinkle on some cake-decorating sugar sprinkles to look like the gooseberries. Since you can't fit 10 candles on each cake, put one candle on each instead.

EDIBLE AQUARIUMS to go with *Swimmy* by Leo Lionni, Knopf: ISBN 0394817133 (hc), 0394826205 (pbk).

■ Swimmy joins forces with all the other little fish to outwit the predators. No sharks are lurking in these little oceans of delectable snacking.

Ingredients
1 package blue Jell-O®
1 package Pepperidge Farm® Goldfish® crackers
lettuce leaves (optional as seaweed)

Other
12 clear plastic drink cups

Directions
Make blue Jell-O according to package directions and put into clear drink cups. Refrigerate. Poke a hole in the cold Jell-O with a finger (wash your hands first!), and then put a goldfish in the "aquarium." You can do this over and over. If you want to add aquarium plants, use lettuce leaves slithered into the Jell-O with a knife.

SPROUT SANDWICHES to go with *Sylvester and the Magic Pebble* by William Steig, Simon & Schuster: ISBN 067166154X (hc), 0671662694 (pbk).

■ Sylvester is having a picnic. As he nibbles on a sprout sandwich, Sylvester is rudely turned into a rock by a witch who needs to get a life.

Ingredients
12 slices bread
1 stick butter (or use the **Homemade Butter** recipe included to go with Sam and the Tigers)
1 package alfalfa sprouts

Directions
Spread each slice of bread with butter. Sprinkle with alfalfa sprouts. Fold bread and eat. Caution: Do not wish on red pebbles while eating!

DELIGHTFUL CUT-UP SNACK to go with the story of "Bad Mousie" in *The Tall Book of Make-Believe* by Jane Werner, illustrated by Garth Williams, Harper & Row.

■ Bad Mousie uses scissors to cut up the quilt and make a mess. Donica teaches him to cut other things with scissors and stay out of trouble. Cutting up all these ingredients will keep kids out of trouble for a while too. Make sure the scissors are clean.

Ingredients
1 package dried apricots
1 package dried apples
1 package dried prunes
1 package dried peaches
1 package dried pineapple
1 package dried figs
1 package dates
1 package raisins
1 package cashews
1 package almonds

Directions
Using clean scissors, have children cut all the ingredients into little pieces and put in a large bowl. After all the cutting us complete, mix the ingredients together and distribute into paper cups for a snack.

BIG TOE-PRINT COOKIES

to go with *Those Toes* by Marie McLaughlin, illustrated by Roni Rohr, Azro Press: ISBN 1929115016 (hc).

■ The story is all about the variety and joys of toes. These are big, giant toe-print cookies.

Ingredients

2/3 cup margarine	1/2 teaspoon salt
1/3 cup sugar	1 1/2 cups flour
2 egg yolks	2 egg whites slightly beaten
1 teaspoon vanilla	almonds

Directions

Cream margarine and sugar until fluffy. Add egg yolks, vanilla, and salt, beat well. Add flour gradually to blend thoroughly. Shape into 1-inch oval shapes, press thumb deeply into one end of oval. Brush with beaten egg white. Place cookies 1 inch apart on ungreased cookie sheet. Bake at 350°F for 10-13 minutes. Cool slightly before removing from cookie sheet. Place one of the following in the indentation: a cherry or a teaspoon of jam to represent a painted toenail, or an almond to represent an unpainted toenail. Contributed by Marie McLaughlin.

MONKEY BANANA MUFFINS WITH CHOCOLATE CHIPS to go

with *Those Toes* by Marie McLaughlin, illustrated by Roni Rohr, Azro Press: ISBN 1929115016 (hc).

■ *Those Toes* offers interesting illustrations of the feet and toes of different animals, including monkeys.

Ingredients

1/2 teaspoon sugar	1/4 cup milk
1 teaspoon baking soda	3 medium bananas mashed
1/4 teaspoon salt	1 teaspoon vanilla
3/4 cup flour	1/3 cup raisins or cran-raisins
3/4 cup whole wheat flour	1/3 cup milk chocolate chips
1/3 cup oil	

Directions

Use nonstick cooking spray in your muffin cups or use cupcake papers. Preheat oven to 375°F. Combine sugar, baking soda, salt, and both flours in a big bowl. Combine oil, milk, bananas, and vanilla in a separate bowl. Mix dry and wet ingredients together and add raisins and chocolate chips. Pour into muffin cups and bake 11 minutes. Contributed by the author.

COYOTE STEW to go with
Three Little Javelinas by
Susan Lowell, illustrated
by Jim Harris, Rising
Moon: ISBN 0873585429
(hc).

■ The evil coyote is cooked into a stew by the resourceful
three little pigettes who are desert female javelinas of infinite
resourcefulness.

Ingredients
1 package beef stew cubes
1 can beef broth
1 carrot, sliced thinly
1 stalk celery, sliced thinly
1 handful potato chips crushed
1 turnip, sliced thinly
1 apple, sliced thinly
1 jicama, peeled and sliced thinly
1 zucchini, sliced thinly

Directions
Combine all ingredients in a crock-pot and let it bubble away
for about an hour.

PIGS IN A BLANKET to go
with *The Three Little Pigs*
by James Marshall,
Dutton: ISBN
0803705913 (hc).

■ These traditional little treats are easy to make.

Ingredients
1 package Little Smokies sausages
1 can refrigerated croissants (sliced into smaller triangles so there
  is one "blankie" per piggy)

Directions
Wrap each little piggy in a slice of a croissant, tucking the end under
the piggy. Bake on a cookie sheet at 350°F for about 12 minutes or
until the dough starts to brown.

EDIBLE PIGGIES SNACK to
go with *The Three Little Wolves and the Big Bad Pig* by Eugene Trivizas, illustrated by Helen Oxenbury, Econo-Clad: ISBN 0613021339 (hc), Aladdin 0689815284 (pbk), Margaret McElderry: 0689505698 (lb). You could also use this recipe with the story "Ashes" in *The Devil's Storybook* by Natalie Babbitt, Econo-Clad: 0613134486 (hc), Farrar, Straus, and Giroux: 0374417083 (pbk).

■ When you get a bad piece of pork, the only thing to do is make deviled ham treats. Both of these stories are about "bad pigs."

Ingredients
2 cans deviled ham
6 white flour tortillas
1 can chowmein noodles

Directions
Spread deviled ham on tortillas. Add "bones" or chowmein noodles, roll up in tortillas, cut in half and serve.

THIRD LITTLE PIG'S DINNER to go with *The Three Pigs* by Paul Galdone, Clarion: ISBN 0395288134 (hc), 0899192750 (pbk).

■ Bubbling away in a pot on the fire, this "wolf-jerky" dinner will warm any little piggy heart.

Ingredients
1 package beef jerky
12 carrots
2 large potatoes
2 teaspoons Italian seasoning or oregano
1 cans tomato soup
2 cans water

Directions
Cut the beef jerky with scissors into pieces the size of a penny. This is the "wolf" for the stew. Cut carrots into "coins"—the thinner they are sliced the faster they cook. Wash potatoes, slice and dice (no need to peel). In a large crock-pot, combine jerky, carrots, potatoes, seasoning, and soup. Add water. Kids might want to cut up onions and "cry" over the death of the wolf, or you can cheat and use dried onion flakes or onion salt if your hard-hearted little piggies don't want to mourn the wolf. Cook all day, let sit one night, and eat the next day.

THUNDERING GOOD THUNDERCAKE to go with

Thundercake by Patricia Polacco, Philomel: ISBN 0399222316 (lb).

■ The little girl in the story is afraid of thunderstorms, so her grandmother diverts her attention from the storm by making this cake.

Ingredients

1 cup shortening
2 cups sugar
1 teaspoon vanilla
3 eggs
1 cup cold water
1/3 cup pureed tomatoes
2 1/2 cups flour

1/2 cup Hershey's baking cocoa
1 1/2 teaspoons baking soda
1 teaspoon salt
one can ready-made chocolate icing
one small tube of decorator icing
   (white or silver)

Directions

Cream shortening, sugar, vanilla, and eggs together. Add tomatoes and water. Stir well. In a separate bowl, sift together flour, cocoa, baking soda, and salt. Mix wet mixture and dry mixture together. Pour into cupcake papers in cupcake pans. Bake at 350°F for 25 minutes. Cover with chocolate icing then make a lightning bolt on each cupcake with white or silver icing.

CHICKEN CATERPILLARS

to go with *Toe Stomper and the Caterpillars* by Sharleen Collicott, Houghton Mifflin: ISBN 0395911680 (hc).

■ A Bully would be smitten with these cute little caterpillars. The recipe could be used with any caterpillar book, including *Charlie the Caterpillar* by Dom Deluise, illustrated by Christopher Santoro, Simon & Schuster: ISBN 0671693581 (lb).

Ingredients

4 precooked chicken breasts
   (cubed into 48 pieces or
   four pieces per child)
1 red bell pepper (cored, seeded,
   and cut into little triangles)

12 fresh mushrooms
2 fresh zucchini (cut into "coins")
1 bunch green onion tops
1 pint cherry tomatoes
sunflower seed kernels (for eyes)

Other

12 wooden skewers

Directions

Use the ingredients to make shish kebabs, and assemble "caterpillars." Use cherry tomatoes for the heads, and onion tops for the tails. Nuke on paper plates for about two minutes. Let cool before eating.

PANETTONE to go with
Tony's Bread: An Italian Folktale by Tomie dePaola, Putnam: ISBN 0399216936 (hc), PaperStar 0698113713 (pbk).

■ Traditionally this bread is made in a flowerpot, with pieces of citron and various dried fruits.

Ingredients
1 box bread mix, any flavor
1 handful chopped dried raisins
1 handful chopped citron
1 handful chopped candied cherries
1 brand-new 8-inch red, clay flowerpot
nonstick cooking spray

Directions
Use a bread maker and any boxed bread mix (use the DOUGH setting for about an hour and a half). When the dough is done with its first rise, take it out and knead it, Add cut candied fruit, raisins, and other dried fruit at this point. Knead them into the dough well. Place dough in a flowerpot that has been coated with nonstick cooking spray. Let the dough rise one more time. Bake at 350°F for one hour. Tap on the top to see if it's done. When it's ready, it sounds hollow and is all brown and pretty.

TAMALE PIE to go with
Too Many Tamales by Gary Soto, illustrated by Ed Martinez, Putnam/PaperStar: ISBN 0698114124 (paperback), 0399221468 (lb).

■ After making lots of tamales, one of the girls discovers she has lost a ring off her finger and has to eat too many tamales in order to find it. If she had made tamale pie, she could have just poked around with a fork until she found the ring. You could divide the steps in this recipe so the students work with partners to add one ingredient each.

Ingredients
1 medium bag of tortilla chips
1 can chili
1 cup grated cheese

1 can corn, drained
2 cups shredded lettuce
1 can chopped green chili

Directions
Put tortilla chips in the bottom of a 9x14-inch glass dish. Spread chili over chips. Add a layer of corn. Add a layer of cheese. Nuke it at 50% until the cheese melts (if you nuke it at full blast the cheese will get rubbery). Serve hot.

FOREST LOGS to go with *The Tree in the Ancient Forest* by Carol Reed-Jones, illustrated by Christopher Canyon, Dawn Publications: ISBN 1883220327 (hc), 1883220319(pbk).

■ Large fallen trees (like the 300-year-old tree in the book) make good shelter for many forest creatures and are an important part of the ancient forest. Enjoy these edible logs.

Ingredients
4 cups finely chopped dried fruit (raisins, apricots, figs, pitted dates, pitted prunes, and so on)
1 cup finely chopped nuts
2 to 4 tablespoons honey or water
roasted carob powder to thicken (optional)

Other
toothpicks

Directions
Cut the fruit and nuts into small pieces using knife or scissors. Blend the dried fruit, nuts, and honey together by hand to make a thick dough. If it is too dry, add a little extra honey or water a teaspoon at a time until the mixture forms into a thick dough. Roll into log shapes and use a toothpick to make stripes that look like bark.
Contributed by Carol Reed-Jones.

FOREST TEA to go with *The Tree in the Ancient Forest* by Carol Reed-Jones, illustrated by Christopher Canyon, Dawn Publications: ISBN 1883220327 (hc), 1883220319 (pbk).

■ One can make tea from the leaves of two trees that grow in the Pacific Northwest forests—Douglas Fir (Pseudotsuga menziessii) and Western Hemlock (Tsuga heterophylla). The Western Hemlock is NOT the same as Poison Hemlock (Conium maculatum), which is deadly. You could combine this recipe with a trip to a tree nursery or forest ranger station.

Ingredients
12 Douglas Fir or Western Hemlock twigs
hot water

Directions
Gather Douglas Fir or Western Hemlock twigs with fresh needles from unsprayed trees that are NOT near a road. Use twigs that are about 4 to 6 inches long. Rinse with running water and pat dry with a clean towel. Pull off the needles and put them into a teapot. Heat water to boiling and carefully pour it into the teapot. Let the needles steep for about five to 10 minutes, then pour tea through a strainer into teacups or mugs. You may sweeten it with honey if you like. This tea tastes piney because both Douglas Fir and Western Hemlock are members of the pine family. Contributed by Carol Reed-Jones.

A. WOLF'S SUGARLESS BIRTHDAY CAKE to go with *The True Story of the Three Little Pigs* by Jon Scieszka, illustrated by Lane Smith, Viking/Puffin: ISBN 0670827592 (hc) 0140544518 (pbk).

■ Mr. Alexander T. Wolf claims he only went to get sugar for a cake for his poor old granny and that's how the pig "accident" happened. Likely story. Here's his recipe for sugarless cake, as if that proves anything!

Ingredients
1 package yellow cake mix
1 large package instant vanilla pudding
4 beaten eggs
3/4 cup vegetable oil
3/4 cup beverage (7 UP, Coke, root beer, and so on)
1 teaspoon nutmeg

Directions
Combine ingredients in a bowl. Mix for five minutes with electric mixer or by hand. Pour into a greased baking pan (a Bundt pan works nicely). Bake at 375°F for 45-60 minutes or until inserted wooden skewer comes out clean. Cool in pan for about five minutes before turning out onto rack.

BIRD PIE to go with
The Twits by Roald Dahl,
illustrated by Quentin
Blake, Puffin: ISBN
0141301074 (pbk).

■ The Twits are the most reprehensible people on the planet. This is one of their favorite treats because of the little bird feet sticking up out of the crust. Gross.

Ingredients
1 pie with a solid top crust (purchase any kind)
1 bag of pretzel sticks
peanut butter

Directions
Using peanut butter as "glue," make "bird feet" with pretzel sticks. Attach the bird feet on the top of the pie and serve.

ANTS ON A LOG to go
with *Two Bad Ants* by
Chris Van Allsburg,
Houghton Mifflin: ISBN
0395486688 (hc).

■ This traditional snack could be used with any ant books, including *The Ant and the Elephant* by Bill Peet, Houghton Mifflin: ISBN 0395169631 (hc), 0395292050 (pbk); *The Ants Go Marching* by Mary Luders, illustrated by Geoffrey Hayes, HarperFestival: 0694014478 (hc); or *One Hundred Hungry Ants* by Elinor Pinczes, illustrated by Bonnie MacKain, Houghton Mifflin: 0395971233 (pbk), 0395631165 (lb). If you use it with the Pinczes story, line up the celery sticks so the hungry ants don't have to wait in line to eat.

Ingredients
12 sticks celery
1 container cream cheese
raisins

Directions
Wash and clean celery. Spread cream cheese into the hollow place in celery. Place raisin "ants" on the cream cheese.

LEMON MOON COOKIES

to go with *Under the Lemon Moon* by Edith Hope Fine, illustrated by René King Moreno, Lee and Low: ISBN 1880000695 (hc), Spanish Edition: 1880000903 (hc).

■ These lemony cookies resemble yellow moons.

Ingredients
6 tablespoons shortening
3/4 cup sugar
3 tablespoons milk
1 egg
2 teaspoons baking powder
1/4 teaspoon salt
1 1/2 cups flour
2 tablespoons lemon juice
2 teaspoons grated lemon rind

Directions
Preheat oven to 375°F. Cream shortening and sugar. Add milk, egg, baking powder, salt, and flour. Mix well. Add lemon juice and rind. Mix well. Drop by teaspoonfuls 2 inches apart on greased cookie sheet. Bake 10-15 minutes until cookies are a light golden brown. Contributed by Edith Hope Fine.

CHOCOLATE-COATED BUGS

to go with *The Valentine Bears* by Eve Bunting, illustrated by Jan Brett, Clarion: ISBN 089919138X (hc), 0899193137 (pbk).

■ Mr. and Mrs. Bear never get to celebrate Valentine's Day because they're hibernating, so Mrs. Bear sets her alarm for February and surprises her sweetie with these yummy treats before they both settle back for a few months' more sleep.

Ingredients
1 bag chocolate chips
1 box Kix® cereal
butter (for hands)

Directions
Nuke the chocolate chips in a heat-resistant dish at 50% until melted. Mix Kix into chocolate, one handful at a time until the cereal is evenly coated. Butter hands lightly. Take a small handful of the cereal mix. Roll out golf-ball-sized treats. Cool on wax paper. Enjoy.

EDIBLE METAMORPHIC PASTA to go with *The Very Hungry Caterpillar* by Eric Carle, Putnam: ISBN 0399208534 (hc), Philomel: 0399226907 (board book).

■ Tracing the metamorphic cycle of butterflies using various pasta forms may not be good science, but it's good eating.

Ingredients

12 bow tie pasta, cooked
12 fusilli pasta cooked
cocoa
cake sprinkles
butter

Directions

After you cook the pasta, keep each kind separate. Toss with butter to coat the warm noodles. Each child needs a separate white paper plate to make butterflies and caterpillars. Coat the fusilli with cocoa mix to make them brown and fuzzy. Coat the bow ties with sparkly cake sprinkles to make them beautiful. Eat the caterpillars and butterflies with a toothpick.

PANCAKE AND SAUSAGE CATERPILLAR BUTTERFLIES to go with *The Very Hungry Caterpillar* by Eric Carle, Putnam: ISBN 0399208534 (hc), Philomel: 0399226907 (board book).

■ Make these adorable little edible insects to accompany any caterpillar book.

Ingredients

12 precooked link sausages
12 pancakes in butterfly-wing shapes (or use a heart-shaped cookie cutter)
jelly
squirt icing (any kind)
licorice shoestrings
raisins

Directions

Place butterfly-wing pancakes on plate, using sausage as the body of the butterfly. Decorate the wings with jelly and squirt icing. Add two feelers made out of licorice shoestrings with raisins at the tip.

A TRANSFORMATIVE FEAST to go with *The Very Hungry Caterpillar* by Eric Carle, Putnam: ISBN 0399208534 (hc), Philomel: 0399226907 (board book).

■ Before the caterpillar metamorphoses, it indulges in a huge eating binge. Tiny butterfly-sized bites of all these goodies will help students re-enact the feast.

Ingredients

dried apples
fresh strawberries
dried pears
dried plums
chocolate cupcake
pickles
slices of Swiss cheese

slices of salami
one lollipop (smashed with a hammer)
candied cherries
fresh orange
sausage or bratwurst
watermelon
ice cream dots (freeze-dried ice cream)

Directions

Cut each item into at least 12 pieces (for 12 students to taste). Put each on paper plates. Students can eat each treat blindfolded or in the dark and guess what it is. After they eat one taste of everything, maybe they'll turn into butterflies!

FOU FOU to go with *The Village of Round and Square Houses* by Ann Grifalconi, Little Brown: ISBN 0316328626 (hc).

■ "Fou Fou" is eaten at every meal in the story. It's sort of like white poi (the Hawaiian equivalent of edible wallpaper paste).

Ingredients

2 cups quick grits or Cream of Wheat® (cook with water, according to directions)
sugar to taste

Directions

Cook grits or Cream of Wheat in water until thickened. If you like, you could serve this "fake fou fou" in hollowed-out potato skins, orange rinds, lemon rinds, or even on a "boat" of a watermelon rind.

ICE CREAM IN A BAG

to go with *We All Scream for Ice Cream!: The Scoop on America's Favorite Dessert* by Lee Wardlaw, illustrated by Sandra Forrest, HarperTrophy: ISBN 0380802503 (pbk).

■ Children can make this ice cream with little fuss or muss, and it's delicious! You don't need an ice cream machine, and you don't need a freezer for hardening or storage, so you can make this just about anywhere.

Ingredients
For each child you'll need:
1/2 cup heavy whipping cream
1 tablespoon sugar
1/4 teaspoon vanilla extract
2 cups ice cubes
6 tablespoons rock salt

Other
1 Ziploc® brand sandwich bag
1 Ziploc freezer bag (quart size)
1 pair oven mitts
1 dish towel
1 spoon

Directions
Pour the cream into the sandwich bag. Add the sugar and vanilla to the same bag. Seal the bag, making sure it is tightly closed; otherwise the ingredients will leak. Place the closed sandwich bag inside the freezer bag. Pour the ice into the freezer bag. Pour the rock salt into the freezer bag. Seal the freezer bag, tightly. Put on the oven mitts or wrap the dish towel loosely around the freezer bag. Shake, rock, roll, and squeeze the bag for a full five minutes. Note: the bag is going to get very cold, 18°F-20°F. The mitts or dish towel will keep your hands from freezing. Open the freezer bag and remove the sandwich bag. Using the dish towel, quickly wipe away any rock salt and water from the outside of the sandwich bag. The ice will have almost completely melted, so the outside of the sandwich bag will be wet. This will keep the salt and water out of the sandwich bag—and the ice cream—when you open it. Open the sandwich bag and enjoy! Eat the ice cream right out of the bag or spoon it into a bowl. To remove every last delicious bit of the ice cream, turn the bag inside out and scrape the sides with a spoon. Try drizzling chocolate sauce or some other syrup on top of the ice cream, along with sprinkling chocolate chips, M&M's, granola, nuts or other toppings over it. You could also mix it with fresh strawberries, raspberries, blueberries, or peaches. Contributed by Lee Wardlaw.

BRUNCH CASSEROLE

from *We're Making Breakfast for Mother* by Shirley Neitzel, illustrated by Nancy Winslow Parker, Greenwillow: ISBN 0688145752 (hc).

■ When the children make breakfast for their mother, they have the best intentions, but breakfast doesn't turn out quite the way they had planned. Nevertheless, Mother is pleased.

Ingredients
6 slices bread
12 smoky links
2 cups shredded cheese
3 eggs
2 cups milk

Directions
Coat a 9x13-inch baking pan with nonstick cooking spray. Tear bread into small pieces and place in pan. Slice sausages into penny-sized pieces and scatter over the bread. Cover sausage with shredded cheese. Mix together eggs and milk. Pour over cheese. Bake at 350°F for 45-60 minutes. If you like, you could serve the casserole with fresh fruit. Contributed by Shirley Neitzel.

WHEN THE WATER CLOSES OVER MY HEAD SANDWICHES to go with *When the Water Closes over My Head* by Donna Jo Napoli, illustrated by Nancy Poydar, Puffin: ISBN 0525450831 (pbk).

■ When the main character in the story makes sandwiches for his family, it leads to funny things.

Ingredients
2 cans tuna
mayonnaise
black olives, sliced
chopped carrots
bread for making sandwiches

Directions
Mix tuna with mayonnaise, olives, and carrots, then spread on bread, and enjoy. Contributed Donna Jo Napoli.

MAX'S WILD RUMPUS SUPPER to go with *Where the Wild Things Are* by Maurice Sendak, HarperCollins: ISBN 0060254920 (hc), 0060254939 (lb).

■ Max gets sent to bed without supper then partakes in a wild adventure. When he returns, his supper is still hot. This recipe stays hot even when it's cold outside.

Ingredients
1 can tomatoes
1 can kidney beans
1 can garbanzo beans
1 can olives
1 teaspoon dried chopped onions
1 small can green chili chopped

Directions
Combine ingredients in a crock-pot and cook for about three hours. It will still be hot when Max gets home, guaranteed.

WILD JIGGLERS to go with *Where the Wild Things Are* by Maurice Sendak, HarperCollins: ISBN 0060254920 (hc), 0060254939 (lb).

■ When the Wild Things have their wild rumpus, they certainly shake things up and jiggle things around, so these treats would be great to serve at your wild rumpus party.

Ingredients
4 small packages of Jell-O®
2 cups boiling water
1 cup cold milk
1 package Jell-O instant vanilla pudding mix

Other
animal-shaped cookie cutters

Directions
Pour Jell-O in bowl, dissolve in hot water. Cool to room temperature. Pour 1 cup cold milk and 1 package Jell-O instant vanilla pudding mix into a container with a tight lid and shake. Then pour the pudding mixture into the gelatin mixture. Stir together and pour into 9x13 pan. Chill three hours. After it's set, dip the bottom of the pan in warm water 15 seconds. Then cut out jigglers with cookie cutters shaped like animals.

WILD WILLIE GLOP from *Wild Willie and King Kyle*: *Detectives* by Barbara Joosse, illustrated by Sue Truesdell, Clarion: ISBN 0395643384 (hc), Dell: 0440411076 (pbk).

■ Wild Willie plans to make "glop" with his best friend, Kyle. They like to be gross, and it's the kind of thing best friends do. This is their secret formula, but you can add other stuff if you like.

Ingredients
warm water
skunk cabbage
hot sauce
sugar
dandelion fuzz
chocolate syrup

Directions
First mix skunk cabbage with warm water. Then stir in hot sauce and sugar. Next add dandelion fuzz and chocolate syrup. Put it in the sun until it's gross. Bury it. Dig it up. Contributed by Barbara Joosse.

PUMPKIN SQUARES

to go with *Winter Lullaby* by Barbara Seuling, illustrated by Greg Newbold, Harcourt Brace: ISBN 0152014039 (hc).

■ This story brings to mind that time of year when creatures look for warmth and shelter away from the cold. The season begins with the harvest, when big, orange pumpkins dot the countryside, and the smell of pumpkins baking in pies and puddings fills the air. This cozy addition to the table would be a nice snack or treat after pumpkin picking.

Ingredients
3 cups gingersnap cookie crumbs
1/3 cup melted margarine
3 8-ounce packages cream cheese (softened)
1 1/2 cups sugar
3 eggs separated
1 teaspoon vanilla
1 16-ounce can pumpkin
1 1/2 teaspoon pumpkin pie spice
1 12-ounce can evaporated milk
Cool Whip® or whipped cream

Directions
Mix cookie crumbs and margarine. Press into 9x13-inch baking pan. Beat cream cheese with electric mixer on medium speed until smooth. Add 3/4 cup sugar, two eggs, and vanilla. Mix until blended, and then pour over crust. Beat remaining one egg in separate bowl, and then stir in pumpkin, remaining 3/4 cup sugar, and pumpkin pie spice. Gradually stir in evaporated milk. Pour over cream cheese layer. Bake at 375°F for one hour until set. Cool. Refrigerate until ready to serve. Top with Cool Whip or whipped cream and sprinkle with additional cookie crumbs. Contributed by Barbara Seuling, who says she got this yummy recipe from her friend Roseann Palma.

FAKE SUSHI to go with
Yoko by Rosemary Wells,
Hyperion: ISBN
0786803959 (hc)

■ Yoko takes real sushi to school for lunch and is shunned by the straight-laced non-gourmands in her class.

Ingredients
12 slices turkey lunch meat
2 cups cooked rice
red jelly or cranberry sauce

Directions
Spread a thin layer of rice on the turkey slice. Add a "line" of jelly or cranberry sauce so when you roll up the sushi roll, each piece you cut off will have a red center. To roll sushi, you use a bamboo mat that packs and compacts the rice. If you don't happen to have one, you can roll up the turkey slice on a piece of paper, which also contains any runaway rice. Cut slices of "sushi" with clean scissors and let each slice "set" in the refrigerator for a while.

LEMON PIE to go with
Zilla Sasparilla and the Mud Baby by Judith Gorog, illustrated by Amanda Harvey, Candlewick Press: ISBN 1564022951 (hc).

■ Everybody in the village goes to old Granny Vi for advice. When Zilla goes one night for a bit of counsel, Granny Vi feeds her lemon pie and coffee.

Ingredients
1 box Nilla® wafers
1 stick butter
1 can lemon pie filling

Directions
To make instant lemon pies, grind up a box of Nilla wafers in a food processor. Add a stick of butter and mix it until it's sort of the consistency of cat litter. Press this "crust" into each cup of a 12-hole muffin tin and fill the "pie crust" with premade lemon pie filling. Let it set in the refrigerator until firm. Then each youngster can have a little lemon pie and a cup of coffee.

CHEESE SNACKS from *Zilla Sasparilla and the Mud Baby* by Judith Gorog, illustrated by Amanda Harvey, Candlewick Press: ISBN 1564022951 (hc).

■ In the story, everyone in the village goes to see Granny Vi for advice—and cheese snacks.

Ingredients

2 sticks butter
2 cups unbleached flour
1 8-ounce package of cream cheese or farmer's cheese
grated cheese such as Parmesan, Romano, Gruyère, or dry
    Swiss cheese
1 egg beaten
a pinch of salt (if you use unsalted butter)

Directions

Moosh together butter, flour, and cream cheese. Knead, pat out until it is about 1/2-inch thick. Then fold over as many times as you can. Let dough rest about 30 minutes. Roll or pat out, and cut into circles with a small jelly glass, souvenir shot glass, or small biscuit cutter. The larger they are, the longer they take to bake. When all the dough has been cut into circles press the top of each one in a tic-tac-toe pattern with the tines of a fork. Brush the top with the beaten egg and sprinkle a few bits of grated cheese onto the egg. The egg is the glue to keep the cheese on the top. Place a baking sheet and slide into preheated 350°F oven. Bake 18-22 minutes. Let cool. The snacks come from the oven very hot inside.
Contributed by Judith Gorog.

Index

About the Author

Gwynne Spencer has been a teacher, children's bookseller, puppeteer, storyteller, newspaper columnist, editor, and is now a full-time writer. She lives and works in Mancos, Colorado near Mesa Verde National Park not far from the Four Corners. She has two grown children, three fierce little dachshunds, and is looking for some smart chickens, a Palomino horse and a Guernsey cow to round out her bucolic existence planting and harvesting herbs on 20 acres along the Mancos River.

While she's waiting for the plants to grow, she writes a monthly column called "Kids Love Books" which appears in over 100 newspapers nationwide, and writes articles on children, books and reading for many parenting publications, as well as travel articles for a variety of publications. Other books by the author include "Teach Your Children Well: A Guide to Teaching Reading at Home," "Perfect Plots for Mere Mortals: A Writer's Quick Guide to the Hero Journey," "Places to Go with Children in the Southwest," "The Ultimate Family Guide to New Mexico (with Nanette Ely-Davies)," and "Instant Science Projects."

Gwynne grew up in Abington, Pennsylvania, attended Beaver College in nearby Glenside, PA and then moved to New Mexico where she lived in Albuquerque for many years. During that time, she taught various ages and grades. In 1977 she opened Trespassers William children's bookstore, where she enjoyed selling and reading children's books, meeting authors, sponsoring storytelling events and giving kid's workshops, many of which involved cooking and books.

Gwynne hopes readers of *What's Cooking in Children's Literature* will write to her with comments, suggestions and ideas. Gwynne looks forward to attending many state library conferences and sharing culinary adventures with those who love to cook up reading excitement. Contact Gwynne at PengwynneS@aol.com.